Living as Art: 16 Celestial Degrees

Debbie Castle and Judy Johnson
2018

Edits: Teri Crawford and Anthea Church
Cover Design: Judi Rich

ISBN-13: 978-1541114395
ISBN-10: 1541114396

To the Creator,

the Supreme Artist

Appreciations

This jewel of a book outlines a practical exploration of one's inner landscape with the potential for meaningful learning suitable for an individual journey or for a study group. Indeed, this book itself is a work of art.

Judy and Debbie bring many years' experience as educators, facilitators and spiritual teachers to this beautiful book guiding us in how to bring more grace and meaning to our daily lives. With so much emphasis on achievement in our culture, this book provides a framework that nourishes the soul with 16 Arts for how to live as a human "being" in sync with oneself and others. The SERVE model provides a framework for exquisite exploration of each art with thought provoking questions and exercises. Thank you Judy and Debbie for this gift to the world.

Mara Vizzutti, Leadership Coach and Facilitator

The hands on approach to learning and sharing knowledge never disappoints and always results in participants getting the most out of these sessions as I found to be the case with Judy and Debbie's A-Z Virtue Series. Every session produced remarkable results and wonderful, enjoyable break-throughs and surprises. It is well worth your time and effort to go through the series. I expect you'll find, as I did, that the learning is sustained and exponential for you and all the students. I recommend it highly and look forward to Judy and Debbie's next offering with great anticipation.

Ananta Alva, BK Coordinator, Haiti

The Arts of Living described in this book provide a template for inner growth. This book is a catalyst for contemplation that is not prescriptive. It also provides ideas, exercises, questions and commentary that can be used in a group setting. Debbie and Judy have many years' experience facilitating learning and these sessions are rich in their simplicity. They provide a basis for growth and deep knowing. I sincerely hope that you learn as much as I did.

Teri Crawford, Director College Registered Nurses

Many years ago, when I began to meditate, Debbie Castle and Judy Johnson were teaching classes on 26 spiritual virtues. Their book 'The Alphabet Series A-Z' is a culmination of those classes. These virtues are foundational to living a life grounded in a spiritual approach and serve to change internal and external dialogue with self and others. I now teach classes on the spiritual virtues and the book is an invaluable resource. The learning processes suggested for each virtue enable full exploration. I always learn as much and sometimes more than the participants. Thank you, Debbie and Judy for sharing with us.

Janis Brown, Justice of the Peace

Contents

Foreward 9

Introduction 13

The Arts 17

Living as Art: Introductory Session 21

Being Still Inside 29

Thinking 35

Refreshing 41

Sustaining the Self 49

Harmonizing with Others 55

Absorbance 61

Being Happy and Content 67

Communicating 73

Leading 79

Learning and Teaching 85

Revealing and Concealing 91

Moving Forward 97

Serving 103

Transformation 109

Leisure and Work 117

Maintaining Equanimity 123

Celebrating the Arts 131

Back to the Beginning 137

Acknowledgements 139

Resources and Reference Material 141

A List of Virtues 143

Br. Jagdish Chandra ~ 16 Celestial Degrees 145

Anthea Church ~ The Arts of Living 151

Create Your Own 153

Foreword

It is over twenty years since I have thought in depth about the sixteen Arts, as set out in the teachings of the Brahma Kumaris. It is also over twenty years since I read my own writing about these arts and that, too, of Brother Jagdish Chandra.

Inevitably, I find in my own style a florid quality that, as a teacher of English Literature, I would now shun, as well as discourage in my students. However, at the time of writing *The Arts of Living* I was very young, and a regular student with the BKs. The gratitude I feel to their world is profound. When I joined their ranks, I had recently completed a degree at Oxford university under the tutelage of a department of Marxist literary critics for whom there was not only no God but even, it seemed, no self. The BK teachings rescued me from the empty complexity of their world and their students were among the kindest people I have met, either before or since.

I am quite sure that it is with the strength developed from those years spent studying with them, and their immense generosity in offering those teachings at no charge and with such constancy, that I have been able to approach the new phase in my life with more courage and honesty. It would not surprise me, either, if the students who dedicate their lives to the many BK centres all over the world are not also facing more and more profound challenges. After all, the best syllabus ratchets up the tests as the student grows.

It seemed to me then, and still does, a laudable aim to stand up to one's own shortcomings and attempt to transform them, and thus, hopefully, offer also some service to the world. As a lover of art and literature, the notion of oneself as an aspect of creation worthy of being worked on appealed to me greatly and still does.

In my own case, I have come more and more to rely in my own efforts at self-improvement on a robust sense of humour. I have learned this from working for so long with teenagers. What masters they are at diffusing intensity! I have also learned a great deal from reading Shakespeare. He is the genius in terms of understanding the gap between our high-minded aspirations and our irrepressible compulsions. Into that gap springs the endless chaos created by emotion, and that requires delicate handling.

Thus my advice to anyone, whether BK or not, who really wants to master the arts described so sympathetically in this book is to create a community of friends of the kind I so enjoyed during those years. And to talk, share, confess, forgive…

I would also like to pay tribute here to Brother Jagdish. I remember the day that I heard of his death. It struck me with such force that I went for a long run in a wood nearby my small Kentish cottage. As I moved among the trees, weeping, I felt a great closeness to Jagdish as well as a sense that we had both shifted ground for related reasons: to learn new lessons in new places and new ways. Writers must live their words, after all!

For many who read this book, the sixteen arts will be new…a spiritual discovery. For others, they will be familiar ground. What the book does so well is to offer support, wisdom, the invitation to share, as well as suggestions as to how to implement practical change.

I am very grateful to have found myself part of its conception and, in so doing, to have re-encountered Judy Johnson. Her kindness, felt in the quality of her emails, reassures me once more of the deep goodness of the BK family and the nobility of its work.

Anthea Church
1st January 2018

"Although we, as humans, have excelled in numerous forms of art...we are still seeking to learn the art of living." Purity Magazine April 2016

Introduction

"Any normal action that takes on a special degree of attention, expression, finesse and value is an art - a high standard of doing things." Purity Magazine April 2016

Living becomes art when every thought, word and action is an expression of spiritual fullness.

Artists spend years refining the small actions of their craft. Although a flawless performance appears effortless, mastery requires the consistent repetition of small efforts until they are refined to near-perfection.

Art requires mastery. Our lives are the same.

The quality of a life is the result of small actions consistently repeated day after day for years. This is how we learn to master the daily aspects of living in the world; in bodies and in relationships with others. We learn, we lead, we stay healthy, and we need to refresh ourselves in the physical world.

The expression of mastery is a reflection of 'perfectly balanced actions' that enable our life energy to be used for the self and others at the right time in the right way.

This book takes us back-stage into the artist's studio to explore and refine the subtle shifts of ***awareness and attitude*** that are required to generate the ***actions*** that make living an art. Our daily spiritual practice is the consistent repetition of these small energy refinements, these subtle shifts of awareness that infuse high quality energy into every aspect of living, creating living art.

These subtle refinements are possible when we have God at the other end of a safety harness, holding us up above the turbulent, polarizing energies that swirl beneath us and within us as we attempt to master living now. Then, like a spinning top, we maintain perfect balance with our focus on the point (soul) and the Point (Supreme Soul). When the energy is right, a balanced action follows.

In astrological terms, sixteen celestial degrees refers to the moon when it is at its fullest. Seen from earth, the moon brightens the night sky as the sun illuminates its entire surface. The aim of Raja Yoga, as taught by the Brahma Kumaris, is to become full of virtues and positive energy. Pure spiritual energy fills every aspect of the 'being' when the darkness of the soul is released.

When the human soul is full, complete with all virtues, it shines like the full moon reflecting the light of the spiritual Sun (God) on its entire surface.

When every thought, word and action is filled with this highest spiritual energy; living becomes art.

The ARTS
We first learned about the sixteen Arts of Living from our senior BK Brother Jagdish. As he watched the founder Brahma Baba's daily behaviour, he noticed that each of his practical actions ~ sleeping, eating, talking, walking ~ could be described as an art, effortless, natural and so noble. Br. Jagdish wrote about this behaviour to detail this artful living as the ultimate expression of spiritual completeness.

Inspired by Br. Jagdish, we designed a series of experiential learning sessions in 2009. Together with friends and fellow students at the meditation centre in Halifax, we experimented with the arts to develop our capacity to live fully.

We were also inspired by the beautiful writings of Anthea Church in *The Arts of Living* book. Anthea has graciously offered any or all excerpts of her writing to be included in this book. You will find a list of both Br. Jagdish and Anthea's description of the sixteen arts in the Resources section.

We have synthesized what we consider the best of both author's writings with language that feels relevant to our context and time. They are offered to you as a starting point for further reflection and experimentation.

Is this list of sixteen complete? Could we have chosen others? The list isn't meant to be complete. Completeness is to be found inside each art, and in the perfect balance of all of them. Perhaps we each have our own list of sixteen arts, those parts of living where we strive to feel complete. You may wish to create your own list.

How to Use This Book

This book was written for students of the Brahma Kumaris and other spiritual seekers who are dedicated to bringing values and virtues into their practical lives, to transform their own behaviour and ultimately the world.

The sessions are designed to be done alone, even in a small physical space, or with a group. It would work well with a study group to explore one art per week. Or you could dedicate an hour by yourself each week to explore an art and thereby, create a structured 16 week self-study program.

Each art has been written to include two sections:
1. Contemplative sections for those who desire to read and contemplate the questions using a journal.
2. An experiential session with an activity, or several, designed to explore the art experientially. Each session begins with meditation and closes with a song.

As you read, consider how this art is relevant on your journey to completeness. Ask yourself:

1. *What would it be like/feel like to master this art?*
2. *What do you need to master to live this art?*

We encourage you to make effort to experience as many of the arts and exercises as possible. They are designed as a catalyst for discovery, which can only occur through experimentation. When in a group setting, we have found it adds to the session to read the contemplative section aloud AFTER the experiment and reflection.

The design of the activity sessions is built around the five step SERVE model[1] of experiential learning:
- **S**et an intention for learning
- **E**xperience the Art
- **R**eflect on the experience (become more **AWARE** of the art)
- **V**alue the art (awaken a positive **ATTITUDE** towards the art)
- **E**mbody the art (consider ways to put it in **ACTION**)

At a time when everyone is 'doing' so much, this book is about growing our awareness and attitude of *being* complete, full and whole. Our hope is that you will find your centre point of balance and *become* an artist of living.

We hope you enjoy.
All the best,
Debbie and Judy

P.S. Thank you for your efforts to become the best human being you can be.

"Success is guaranteed!!" said the Sun to the Moon.

---

[1] *Personal correspondence Debbie Castle 2015*

The Arts

The Art of Being Still Inside
Stillness is an art. It requires the practice of rising above the movement and turbulence in the mind and body to conquer the restless compulsion to act.

The Art of Thinking
We create our world based on thoughts. This art is about mastering the ability to review your mental creations, and reclaim the power to create high-quality thoughts that are independent of external influences and align with your true self.

The Art of Refreshing
Refreshing yourself means knowing how to re-set energy at a higher level. It involves stepping out of a mundane or old mindset to relax and generate new energy. Refreshment usually involves silence or fun, anything that helps wash away the debris accumulated during everyday life.

The Art of Sustaining the Self
Sustainable energy is precious. This art involves understanding what it takes to care for your energy and nurture the thoughts, food and activities that are healthy and generate wellness and self-respect.

The Art of Harmonizing with Others
Creating harmony is an art that involves thinking about other people generously and in ways that bring mutual benefit. It involves understanding your own unique part in such a way that you play it well. This saves everyone's energy.

The Art of Absorbance
The soul is a sponge and can learn to absorb that which is meaningful and observe the rest from a safe distance. This art involves the power of concentration and focus to absorb the mind

in positive energy without being distracted by the noise around you or in you.

The Art of Being Happy and Content
Contentment is an expression of deep satisfaction in the soul. It becomes an art when you understand and practise thoughts and actions that produce happiness as their fruit. It means learning to dissociate yourself quickly from anything that leads you away from what is joyous.

The Art of Communicating
Communication becomes art when feeling and speaking are congruent; words are clear and have a benevolent effect. It requires sensitivity to simplicity and clarity, and the capacity to balance saying too much against too little.

The Art of Leading
Leading is an art when the qualities most beneficial to a situation guide conversation and action. A skillful balance of leading and following, together with an absence of ego create an atmosphere where *all* can lead.

The Art of Learning and Teaching
Teaching the self well is the art of learning. Learning and teaching are partners in the dance of discovery. Together they build a bridge between the natural interest to learn and the subject of focus.

The Art of Revealing and Concealing
This art involves knowing when to keep something to yourself and when to reveal it. It requires mastering the subtle aspects of timing, discretion and maturity which make a person trustworthy.

The Art of Moving Forward
Moving forward means mastering the ability to maintain momentum and consistency. It involves an understanding that, to avoid stagnation, effort must be exerted and that sustained effort is best fuelled by love.

The Art of Serving
True serving means mastering the art of giving and receiving. It involves understanding the difference between giving of yourself and allowing God to give through you. When God gives, it changes 'doing for' into empowering someone to do for themselves.

The Art of Transformation
Transformation honours the natural desire of the soul to grow by shedding beliefs and fears that limit new expression. It requires knowing what to let go of, when to move on and how to make something good out of any situation, always trusting that even in the worst situations, there will be something to learn.

The Art of Leisure and Work
Leisure is a state of mind. Work becomes leisure when approached with love and lightness. This art enhances all action by filling it with a light attitude and an expression of pure intention. Hard work becomes a game when played with joy.

The Art of Maintaining Equanimity
To remain neutral in the face of opposing forces requires stability. This art involves mastering the practice of being 'centered'; unmoved by praise or defamation, victory or loss.

Living as Art: Introductory Session

*"What is the aim of spiritual effort?
To become complete, full, whole.*

Sixteen celestial degrees means to be complete, free of vice and completely virtuous.

Being sixteen celestial degrees full means that every action performed is seen as an art. When someone is full in this way, their every activity, their way of looking and moving will be seen as an art.

The activity of souls who have attained the complete stage is seen as a talent and it also becomes a divine activity. Some have the speciality or talent of making those who are crying laugh, some have the art of cleanliness, and some have the talent of a miraculous intellect. When you see a speciality in someone, it is said: This one has this talent.

People watch the talents of others with so much interest. You saw a speciality in the way Brahma Baba moved and spoke. He had the art of sitting, seeing and walking. There was a uniqueness and a speciality in everything he did. His every action was seen as an art in a practical way. Sixteen celestial degrees full means that every activity is visible as a perfect talent. This is known as the complete stage."
Taken from BapDada's Murli

When the moon is full it is said to be sixteen celestial degrees. It is an expression of fullness, completeness. When a jar is full and you shake it, it makes no sound, even if there is movement inside. When you shake a jar that is only partially full, there is splashing and noise. The disturbance made by the shaking is obvious.

This is also true with the soul.

On our spiritual journey, we strive to become soul-conscious, sixteen celestial degrees full. We understand that in our current state, we experience darkness, an absence of power and inner light. It is our aim now to become full of all virtues and qualities. In this way, we reflect the light of the Spiritual Sun, like the full moon.

Light is the result. Light is the effect.
Lightness becomes the experience of living.

To become complete is the outcome of the spiritual journey. Shining God's pure energy (light) into the shadows of the soul activates the beauty and radiance of the soul's core qualities.

Invitation to Contemplate and Write:

- *Recall a time when you felt full, able to express your best? What was the experience like?*
- *When are times that you shake? What triggers you?*
- *What would completeness feel like?*
- *Are there times you feel like you're overflowing and can't contain yourself? When?*
- *What is your aim for yourself on your spiritual journey?*
- *What powers do you require to live in the world today?*
- *What virtues will help you activate your finest qualities?*

Setting an Intention for Learning: To explore the metaphor of the full moon as an expression of spiritual completeness.

Introducing the Session
Welcome to the first session of Living as Art. This series of sixteen sessions (plus intro and closing) will explore the highest human character using the metaphor of the full moon, also known as being '16 celestial degrees' complete.

This metaphor of the full moon is about the times when the entire surface of the moon's face is touched by the light from the sun, reflecting a full orb. This metaphor is also symbolic of the human soul which, when complete, shines and radiates inner light like the full moon.

When the human soul is complete and full of all virtues, the finest qualities shine through every thought, word and action. When bright, we see and experience the complete picture of who we really are. The idea of sixteen celestial degrees represents the highest character of the human soul when complete.

During this session, we will explore the concepts related to the uniqueness of each human soul when experiencing completeness.

Experiencing Completeness
We are using 'art' in this series to depict 'an act done with mastery'.

Think about the various art forms. Make a list e.g. dance, drawing, painting, music, singing, theatre, photography, architecture, etc.

Now choose one you admire. Consider: What makes it art-full? What are the qualities that make that art 'art-full'? (In a group, hear comments.)

Think about what is being expressed in this quote:

> "The sign of completeness and perfection is sixteen celestial degrees – this signifies the complete stage. So sixteen celestial

degrees means whatever actions they perform, each action will be seen as an art. Their every activity, their way of looking and moving will be seen as art." Avyakt BapDada

What would life be like if we lived it artfully? (In group, hear comments.)

There is also the idea of 'seamlessness' in action that when something is complete everything is smooth, without a flaw. Yet the artist knows that behind the scenes there are countless repetitions of small actions to perfect or master the art - a brush stroke, a note, harmony, the perfect finger or mouth positioning on an instrument, etc. We understand that 10,000 hours of 'right' effort is required to become a master of that artfulness.

To be a master means to have all the skills, attitudes, talents and awareness required to perform the art flawlessly. It is not just skill. It also involves the right mindset, attitude, awareness and approach.

Imagine for a moment having mastered the skills, talents, attitude, awareness and approach to live every aspect of your life artfully. Spiritually we can call this stage 'complete'.

Are there other words to describe this stage of being *complete* or *artful mastery*? (In a group, hear words. Suggestions include: integrated, healed, whole. Affirm any word that connects to the idea of fullness, complete, sixteen celestial degrees full).

Now take a moment and imagine how this completeness would feel inside. Using one post-it note for each word - identify 3 words that describe what it would feel like to experience each of the words: completely centered, balanced, whole, etc. (In a group use all the other words generated to describe this stage.)

Take a clean sheet of paper and place these post-it notes in the center of the page. Next, draw a circle around all the post-it notes and call it your 'circle of protection'. Take a moment to honour each post-it note inside the circle of protection.

Now consider: What draws you out of your circle of protection? Write these 'pulls' outside the circle you have drawn. (in a group, hear comments)

Then consider: What keeps you inside, in touch with your completeness - feeling full and shining bright? Write inside or around the circle of protection.

Reflecting on the Experience (Awareness)
- What does your experience so far suggest about 'being complete – sixteen celestial degrees full'? (hear comments)

Sit with these thoughts as you read this meditation commentary:

The moon
At its fullest
It lights the night sky
Reflecting the rays of the sun
On every part of its surface
Full moon
Harvest moon
Lover's moon
FULL
Times passes
A night or two
Now fullness diminished
It could be full – but is it?
Hard to tell – the loss is not great enough
The contrast too small to discern
A moment's hesitation – confused
Time passes
It is obvious now
Slivered away until a clean cut reveals half of what it was
Light fading, its distinctive shape still draws the eye
The beauty of perfect geometry?
The knowing of what is still there not visible?
The eye adjusts, navigating the night
Accommodating less light
Time passes
A fragment remains

Slim and elegant
The shadow of the whole still apparent
The brilliance of this shard
Cutting its way through the black sky
A symbol of strength, a reminder of past fullness
And then there is nothing
Searching
seeking
waiting
a lost companion
a startling absence
wondering
when?
The journey back begins
With the last part seen and lost
Most familiar
A finger-hold access
To pull apart the curtains of darkness until the light ball is seen again in its entirety
The journey back begins
With stealth
Unerring as it follows the certain steps
Momentum gaining
Until full potential achieved
A coming home
A celebration
A true return
FULL

Valuing Completeness (Attitude)
- Thinking back on the activity, the reflection, and the commentary: What is the value of being full, complete, sixteen celestial degrees? (In group hear comments.)

Embodying Completeness (Action)
- What can you do this week to keep yourself shining, full and stay in the light? Write an intention in your journal.

Closing

Listen to the song *"Imagine"* by Sam Tsui, thinking about everything you have written inside your circle of protection.

Resources and References:
- Song *Imagine* by Sam Tsui
- Paper, post-it notes, pens

Living as Art: Being Still Inside

"At some point, all the horizontal trips in the world stop compensating for the need to go deep, into somewhere challenging and unexpected; movement makes most sense when grounded in stillness. In an age of speed, I began to think, nothing could be more invigorating than going slow. In an age of distraction, nothing could feel more luxurious than paying attention. And in an age of constant movement, nothing is more urgent than sitting still." Pico Iyer, The Art of Stillness

In a world of constant movement, we take so much satisfaction from action that it is sometimes difficult to be still. Yet stillness is a natural balm for the soul, required for true rest. Slowly, as we learn to meditate and focus our concentrated awareness inwards, we begin to take satisfaction from stillness and silence. When this happens, we begin to lose the compulsion to act. Then actions are created by intention rather than compulsion.

Spiritual mastery is learning to take satisfaction from stillness.

Stillness becomes an art when you master the ability to rise above the movement of the body and turbulence in the mind and conquer the compulsion to act imposed by this intense energy.

"The main state of mind now in the world is the wandering state of mind. Thoughts go in many directions and consciousness is fragmented. Stillness is a settled state of mind. Stillness results in concentration which creates the experience of BLISS. Only when still, can we experience the subtle inner state of bliss."
Br. Jagdish Chandra

Sometimes thinking and consciousness are on high alert as you attempt to decipher signals coming in from the five senses and prepare to act quickly if needed. At other times thought energy seems to slow down to observe what is happening inside and outside of you. Both approaches are needed in a world where things aren't always as they seem.

The ability to pace thought energy allows you to respond thoughtfully. Being still enables you to see and truly understand what is required in the present moment.

Stillness is a break from movement. Stillness is an opportunity to discern what is happening inside you and understand the beneath-the-surface dynamics that influence a situation. Stillness serves to regulate activity. Stillness provides respite.

"To be spiritually complete we must master the art of stopping. To know when to start and when to stop is an art.

When learning to drive a car you must learn how to stop the car. You must know when to stop at a red light. One of the arts of driving is knowing how to stop. You must learn to use the brake so you do not bump into anyone. You can only get a license for driving a car providing you know how to stop.

We have to learn the art of stopping negative/wasteful thinking. Up to now our thinking had no brakes, or the brakes were broken and could not be used. We learn meditation to stop our mind when we like. We have been wasting precious energy for nothing. The negative actions that result from negative thinking are the cause of our sorrow and suffering. If we want happiness we must stop negative actions. To stop negative actions, we need to stop negative thoughts." Br. Jagdish Chandra

Invitation to Contemplate and Write:

- *Remember a time when you experienced stillness that had a positive effect on your surroundings. Describe it.*
- *When does your thought energy speed up or slow down?*
- *What/who controls the speed of your thoughts?*
- *When do you need to move your thought energy quickly?*
- *What helps you BE still?*

Setting an Intention for Learning: To remember what it feels like to be still inside.

Introducing Being Still Inside
Here are some quotes about stillness.

"Away from the chatter of the senses, from the restless wanderings of the mind, there is a quiet pool of stillness. The wise call this the highest state of being." Upanishads (c.1000BCE)

"Nothing in all creation is so like God as stillness." Meister Eckhart (c. 1260-1327)

In the eye of the storm there is stillness. Folk wisdom

"Stillness requires courage." Poster art – source unknown

In this session, you will experience stillness of the mind and its contrasting pace of fast thinking and movement.

Experiencing Being Still Inside
Experiment #1
Wherever you are, stand and look across the room. Choose a spot on the other side of the room. Prepare to time yourself and move quickly and in a dignified manner to that spot on the other side of the room. Check how long it took.

Now return to your starting place covering the same distance. However this time take a full three minutes to get there (or at least twice as long if it's a big room). Be alert to when 30 seconds has passed, when one minute has passed, when two minutes have passed, etc. until the full time has passed.

Experiment #2
Take a chime and sound it. Listen until the sound completely disappears. When you can no longer hear it, sound the chime again, this time with the intention of holding the sound inside you for as long as possible.

Reflecting on the Experience (Awareness)
- What was that like?
- What were you aware of in the quality of your thinking during these two crossings?
- When you compare the two chimes, how long did the sound stay with you? What helped you hold the sound longer?
- What else were you aware of during this activity? (In a group hear comments).

Sit with these thoughts as you read this reflective commentary:

Running.
The habit of running rules.
Bodies and minds run towards desires or away from fears and worries.
The mind runs to get something to fill the emptiness inside.
The mind runs to stay warm when hearts have frozen to the pain around them and in them.
The mind runs away from fear.
There is fear everywhere.
So much running.
As the mind runs, the body follows.
Time speeds up as a result.
Time is relative to movement.
Time is movement.
A creation of the human mind to account for the space between actions.
As there are more actions there is less space.
The human mind is so entangled in actions that it has lost its ability to master time.
It's time to stop running.
It's time to stop time.
I choose to move consciousness inside.
Drawing the energies of my mind into a concentrated point of awareness
I reclaim the moment.
I stop time.
Time stops for me.

In this moment, my energy is perfectly balanced, centered, still.
I fill this moment with the power of my concentrated awareness.
I hold stillness.
A reprieve is found in this still moment.
Energy is stored, concentrated.
I am stable, powerful, still, full.
Then slowly I release time.
To move once again at a pace in keeping with the stillness in my mind.
The world benefits.

At this point hold your awareness still for one full minute. (In a group suggest this, then announce when one minute is complete.)

Now focus your awareness on the point – soul conscious awareness. Set a timer for 2 minutes and attempt to hold your focus still on the point for the entire two minutes.
(In a group setting, read the contemplative section of this art.)

Valuing Being Still Inside (Attitude)
- Given your experiences with being still inside in the activity, discussion and reflective commentary ~ what do you value most about being still inside? What are some places and moments in your life where practicing the art of being still inside would add value?

Embodying Being Still Inside (Action)
- How will you experiment with the art of being still inside this week?

Closing
Play the song *In the Stillness* and let God hold your energy still for one full moment.

Resources and Reference
- Timer
- Song: *In the Stillness* by Karen Drucker

Living as Art: Thinking

"When the atmosphere is right, creation can take place. When a mind meets God, something great is created." Anthea Church

Thought is a seed.

The soul is filled with a garden of possibilities. When well-tended, each thought emerges as a flower. It blossoms, flourishes and creates beauty. The art of thinking requires the skill, patience and discerning eye of a gardener to cut back the weeds that threaten to choke the yet-to-be-seen buds.

The quality of your world depends on the quality of your thoughts. Thoughts are filled with beauty when the energy within them is pure. The art of thinking involves learning to discern and choose to create only high-quality thoughts, to master the ability to review your thoughts regularly and reclaim the power to create your own, independent of external influences.

When minds are trapped in the habit of worry and concern, thoughts are rapid, fragmented or polarized. Then there is no peace because the mind is in pieces.

When a soul is spiritually complete, there are few thoughts and those thoughts are quiet and powerful because they are concentrated with pure energy. Then the only thoughts created are those needed for living. Then living is easy and thoughts are light.

Each thought is an energy investment.

Like any investment, supply and demand dictate value. When scarce something becomes very valuable. Commodities such as salt, water, gold have fluctuated in value throughout history depending on the time and context.

An entrepreneur generates wealth by discerning value and investing in it.

An accurate assessment of the current context is needed to discern the value of something. In times of war, peace is valuable. In times of greed, selfless giving is valuable.

Discerning value is the art of thinking.

In times of darkness, light is valuable. At all times, the greatest spiritual value is that which strengthens and frees the human spirit. Like a good investor, it is time to invest energy in seeds of value.

Invitation to Contemplate and Write:

- *Recall a time when your thoughts were few and clear, life felt easy. Tell the story in as few words as possible.*
- *Which type of thinking occupies most of your day?*
- *Which type of thinking provides the maximum benefit? In what situations?*
- *What determines the value of your thoughts?*
- *What is of greatest value to you? How do your thoughts reflect this?*
- *In the world today, what do you think is the scarcest resource? Time? Peace? Humility? Generosity?*
- *As a gardener, how do you manage the inner garden of your mind/thoughts?*
- *As an entrepreneur, how do you discern the quality of your thinking?*

Setting an Intention for Learning: To discern and increase the quality and benefit in your thinking.

Meditation

Introducing the Art of Thinking
All action in this world begins with a thought. But how often do we stop and calibrate our thoughts to increase the quality of the action that follows? This session heightens our awareness of the energy of thought, and the energy it carries through to action.

Many of us are surprised when we take the time to itemize the nature and quality of our thoughts - the repetition, the fuzziness, the wandering. And how different these are from thoughts that inspire, calm, and guide us into new ways of seeing and being.

For many of us, re-filling the mind and intellect with spiritual knowledge uplifts our thinking and guides us to new ways of acting in order to improve our world. It all starts with a thought!

Experiencing the Art of Thinking
In this session, you will explore what happens when 'you think you are in thinking mode'; you will check what happens in the mind by being consciously aware of your thinking in five experiments requiring 5-10 minutes each. (This session may be long so you may want to break it up into two sessions.)

Experiment #1
This first exploration is about taking inventory of our thoughts. Set a stop watch for 3 minutes and watch your thoughts during this time. During the three minutes note in your journal each time a thought arises. Write a word to capture the theme of the thought e.g. money, worry, bird song. After 3 minutes, look at your list, count the number of thoughts you had, group similar themes, count the number of times the same theme came up, and name each category of thoughts.

Experiment #2
List the kind of thoughts you have when you are at your best – what are the themes?

Compare this list with the one above - what similarities do you see on the 2 lists? What connections do you see between the themes on the two lists?

How do you feel about what you see in the two lists?

Our thoughts create our reality.

Experiment #3
Hold a thought in your consciousness. Select a virtue and hold it in your awareness...wear it on your face and in your eyes (vision). Look in to a mirror and hold that thought for 3 minutes. What words describe what you see?

(In a group – get in pairs; take turns looking at the face of a partner. Then offer 3 words to describe what you see in that face.)

In your journal reflect on what's surfacing/ coming out of these 3 experiments in thinking.

Watch the YouTube video *'The Science of Seeing into Being'* which suggests we create our world based on the pictures we see (create) in our minds, revealing how important it is to create positive, constructive thoughts.

Experiment #4
Create a thought about a quality or experience you want to grow in yourself. Note: remember, the mind does not see an image for the word DON'T. When you tell yourself DON'T be angry, the mind sees a picture of angry. So, you must create a positive picture of what you want to be e.g. I want to be peaceful. An even more powerful thought is I AM Peaceful.

'I AM peaceful'/'I am peace' is an assertion of what is true, what is already inside you. Similar to the way the moon is always full, although it is not visible until the sun shines on it.

Select a quality that you would like to shine more brightly. Create a detailed picture in your mind of this quality shining brightly in you. Hold this picture for three minutes.

Experiment #5
Testing what is true in your thinking. Stand balanced and pick a virtue card. Read it, then hold it to your chest, imagine what the virtue feels like inside then silently say to yourself *'I am___ e.g. peace'*.

If it is true the body will rock forward, if it is not true for you at this time the body will lean backward and take you off balance. This is evidence about the work to be done to bring this virtue into manifestation.

(In a group, get into pairs. Have one person extend their arm out to the side, shoulder height parallel to the floor and think a weak thought – 'I don't want to be angry'. The other person places their hand on the wrist of that person and gently pushes down. If the thought is weak, it is easy to push the arm down. Next ask the same person to switch to a powerful thought – I am peace. How much strength is required to push the arm down this time? This is a test of the power of a true thought. Switch and have the other person experiment with the power of a weak thought and a powerful one.

Reflecting on the Experience (Awareness)
- What new awareness do you have about your thinking?
- What are you thinking about your thinking!?
- What moment was especially noteworthy for you among the five experiments? (hear comments)

Valuing the Art of Thinking (Attitude)
- What is most valuable about mastering your thinking or making thinking an art? (hear comments)
- (In a group setting, take this moment to read the contemplative section of this art aloud to the group.)

Embodying the Art of Thinking (Action)
- Given the value of your experience with these thinking experiments, what is one act of thinking you will practice this week to strengthen the art of thinking? (hear comments)

Closing
Complementary song/music to the art.

Resources and Reference:
- Youtube video: *The Science of Seeing into Being*.
- Self-mastery cards or virtue cards (see list of virtues in resource section)
- Stopwatch or accurate clock

Living as Art: Refreshing

"Refreshment for the mind is new energy washing away old thoughts and patterns. Caught up in the small details of everyday living, there is little chance for refreshment. But there is a resource inside of you that can wash over the immediate and bring something different, not take you away, but bring something fresh and new." Anthea Church

We take holidays to step away from our responsibilities. By changing the setting and the view we change the atmosphere. This is refreshing.

The Art of Refreshing is about taking charge of your inner atmosphere and learning to change it ~ at will. You do this by changing the energy inside you, by taking a break from the mundane, and uplifting to a higher frequency.

My attitude of lightness refreshes me.

The mind gets caught in the mundane, especially when it is over-focused on responsibilities. Refreshment is the result of shifting your focus to become lighter.

The Greek philosopher and mathematician Pythagoras wrote of life as a balance of three essential elements; the self, others and the Divine or truth. He defined the Divine as *that which is good for all* or *that which benefits all*. He suggested that health and well-being are a result of the perfect balance of these three elements. Imbalance is caused by over-focus on one element which results in fatigue, heaviness and an unhealthy life.

For example, over-focus on the self makes you heavy or self-absorbed. Then you cut yourself off from others and the Divine. Too much attention on the Divine, at the expense of others and the self, results in fundamentalism.

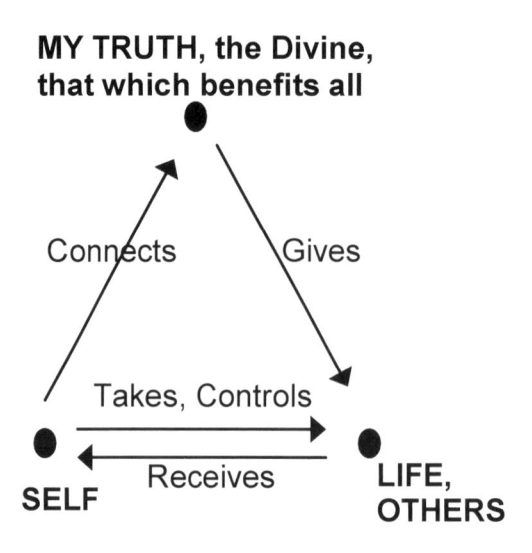

```
        MY TRUTH, the Divine,
        that which benefits all
                 •
               ↗   ↘
         Connects   Gives
         
         Takes, Controls
      •  ─────────────→  •
         ←─────────
          Receives      LIFE,
        SELF            OTHERS
```

A common imbalance in our society is an overemphasis on others. We pay attention to our work, service and children but lose sight of caring for the self. This results in cutting yourself off from your Truth (higher purpose). Another imbalance is caused by wanting something from others. Such desires mean spending time and energy trying to control others in order to get what you want.

For Pythagoras, two of the three elements are naturally and eternally connected. The divine/truth which is good for all will automatically be good for life/others. Therefore, he proposed, the most efficient and effective way to balance your energy is to focus on your higher purpose or calling (your truth, the divine).

Rather than wasting energy trying to control life or to control others, balance and well-being can be attained by understanding your truth. (Your truth not something handed to you by others.)

The way to refresh yourself is to connect with the Divine and uplift your energy to your highest purpose. Because the Divine is already connected to life, it means that life will begin to flow towards you. Pythagoras called this the Divine triangle.

"If we live our life with the definite belief that the Supreme Soul is the real Director and Actor and we are only His instruments, we can always remain contented and relaxed even in illness."
　　　　　　　　　　　Br. Jagdish Chandra

If you understand the magic of this, your life becomes easy, like a dance. You can't imagine the details of how things will work out, but they do. With balance, things just start to happen.

This is the art of refreshing.

Invitation to Contemplate and Write:

- *Remember a time when you kept yourself light while learning and doing meaningful things? Describe how it happened.*
- *What is the quality of your energy today? What has contributed to this?*
- *What are the usual 'conditions' you blame for robbing you of energy?*
- *What strategies or methods do you use to refresh yourself?*
- *Where does God fit in your refreshment plan?*
- *What feels like play for you? How do you play?*
- *How can you carry the feeling of refreshment into everything you do?*
- *In what areas of life would you like to refresh your energy?*

Setting an Intention for Learning: To understand how to reset your energy level and refresh your zeal and enthusiasm in daily activities.

Meditation

Introducing the Art of Refreshing
Three things can help refresh the mind:
1. Trustee Consciousness - letting go of the burden of responsibility. Rather than thinking it is MY responsibility, you develop trustee consciousness. God is here to take the burdens. In what way? When you hold the awareness that it is God's responsibility to get this done ~ through you. With this awareness look up and draw power, strength, clarity and whatever is needed to get the task done. As a child calling upon the Father, hold every responsibility as a trustee - it is not mine.

   When you have a limited capacity to manage, you do everything yourself, you are unable to delegate. Then you get heavy and tired. Spiritual responsibility is to give away thoughts of doubt, worry, fear, smallness and struggle. Being responsible in this way helps you increase your capacity to manage.

2. Connecting to your highest aspirations – they will give you the refreshing energy of higher principles and noble aims.

3. Connecting to God – the source of pure spiritual energy – as the Ocean of Peace, Ocean of Love, Ocean of Bliss…this energy is available to you always.

Experiencing the Art of Refreshing
Three different coloured pieces of paper are needed for this experience.

- On a blue piece of paper - write a responsibility you hold onto, that perhaps feels like a bit of a burden and you would like to feel free from.
- On a pink piece of paper – write one high aspiration you have for yourself.
- On a yellow piece of paper – write a quality of energy you receive when connected in prayer or meditation or silence to the pure source - God.
- Lay the 3 pieces of paper out in front of you in the form of an equilateral triangle. Use the statements you have written to develop sentences into a conversation with God. Add the following starters to the statements you have on the coloured papers.
  - Blue: For the responsibility statement start with "oh woe is me, I must …"
  - Pink: For the highest aspiration, start with "dear soul, come inside and find your deep sense of …"
  - Yellow: For the God statement start with "dear beloved child, remember you can have…"

For a second time, say the full conversation to yourself including the starters. Then let the message sink in and offer some refreshment to your burdened mind!

(In a group, collect all the blue papers and put them in one corner of the room, all the pink ones on another corner of the room and the yellow ones in a third spot in the room that makes an equilateral triangle of the 3 sets of colored paper.

Divide the group in 3 and send each small group to one coloured paper at the points of the triangle. Once there, they are to study all the comments that have been given and develop statements that reflect each unique comment on the pieces of paper, using the format below:

1. Oh woe is me, I must... (the name of a burden of responsibility that requires transformation to trustee consciousness)
2. Dear soul, come inside and find your deep sense of... (write one high aspiration for the self)
3. Dear beloved child, remember you can have... (quality of energy received from God)

The group holding the burdens presents one responsibility in a monologue format – to which both the Aspiration group and the God group will select an appropriate response.

Repeat for each 'burden' held by the Responsibility group. In other words, create a 3-statement conversation using the starters with 1 blue, 1 pink and 1 yellow from each group until all the papers have been read.)

Reflecting on the Experience (Awareness)
Take out your journal:
- How are you feeling after these conversations?
- What stands out as an example of something helpful to the burdened mind?
- What is needed to bring these reminders into your own life of responsibility?
  (Hear comments in a group)

Valuing the Art of Refreshing (Attitude)
- What do you now know and consider true about refreshing yourself and creating new energy in your life? (Hear comments.)

Embodying the Art of Refreshing (Action)
- Take a ribbon and write on it with a marker - one message from your Aspirations or the Divine that will keep you dancing through life! Tie the ribbon around your wrist and wear it this week as a reminder of refreshment.

Closing
Complementary song/music to the art.

Resources and References
- Coloured paper, markers, ribbons for tying around wrist(s).

Living as Art: Sustaining the Self

Sustaining the self is an art when you learn to tap into the sustainable energy at the core of your being. It is precious and must be protected. This requires an intimate understanding of the thoughts, food and activities that are healthy and generate wellness and self-respect.

Each day you keep yourself going by taking care of your body and your health. You can spend years moving from deadline to deadline and from special event to special event, busy, occupied and seemingly content. It may seem like you are sustaining yourself, but eventually you start to feel tired, disheartened or depleted.

The Art of Sustaining the Self is about keeping the spirit deeply nourished. It is about accessing the enduring reservoir of spiritual energy deep inside and allowing it to flow through you like a river of abundance. This nurtures the self and sustains a high quality of life.

"Health (Swasth in Hindi means 'swa' (soul/self). Performing all deeds in a soul conscious stage is the key to be healthy. By considering ourselves as kings of anxiety-less land we can always remain happy because there is no diet comparable to happiness.

Clean drinking water, fresh food and fresh air have an important place in maintaining good health. Baba used to say that for maintaining health and happiness go on earning good wishes of all along with proper meditation and medication. Understanding the deep secret of the drama, and remaining happy in all situations ~ is the art of keeping healthy." Br. Jagdish Chandra

When the spirit is sustained, then the practical details of life take care of themselves. Of course, you must still make appointments, go to meetings and clean the house. When deeply nourished, these tasks become easy and light, not a burden. Paradoxically when you take care of your inner world, your outer world flourishes.

You care lovingly and easily for the physical, practical details at the surface of living by consistently replenishing the deep inner energies of the soul. Your inner and outer worlds are congruent, balanced and your actions are a transparent expression of what is inside you. Your life is a mirror of your inner world.

Spiritual effort means to do what is best for the soul – the eternal being. Thus effort to sustain the soul is effort for the well-being of your whole life.

Invitation to Contemplate and Write:

- *Recall a time when you sustained your energy all day every day for an extended period. What helped you maintain your well-being?*
- *How much attention do you pay to the surface aspects of living?*
- *How much attention do you pay to the deeper aspects of life?*
- *How do your thoughts affect your energy?*
- *What is your source of energy for sustaining yourself?*
- *What is an aim you have for sustaining your 'self' and your well-being?*
- *How would you change your thoughts to sustain yourself and your well-being?*

Setting an Intention for Learning: To discern what is best for sustaining your energy for health and well-being.

Meditation

Introducing the Art of Sustaining the Self
We are inundated with information about what we should and should not do to maintain our well-being. Fads and trends abound about health and wholesome lifestyles. Most are prescriptions for what you should eat, how you should exercise, how you should spend your time at work and in relationships. However, the information they offer changes regularly. You can try them, experiment and judge for yourself what works and doesn't work. However, the foundation assumption behind all these fads is body consciousness ~ that we are bodies.

When you understand that you are a soul, you also understand that your body is a vehicle, meant to carry you to perform actions as you play your unique part in this world. The awareness of self as soul gives you a different starting place for understanding what sustains the 'self'.

You understand that a lack of well-being now is due to the negative actions that have been performed in the past. The karmic residue of these actions weighs heavily on the soul, and ultimately the body. There are habits you must STOP in order for the soul to be well.

In this session, guidance received in Raj Yoga is explored to sustain 'the self' based on the knowledge of soul consciousness. You will specifically look at the suggestions offered us for what *'not to do'* and churn on what can be done instead.

Experiencing the Art of Sustaining the Self
Let's consider some of the DON'T suggestions offered to us in Raj Yoga. For this exploration, use your third eye of knowledge (the divine eye or soul consciousness) to discern what you are being told NOT to do for the well-being of the soul. We are being told what **NOT** to do, and in these cases, it is left up to you to consider what you **CAN** do for your well-being.

To explore what is best for self-sustenance and your own well-being, use this 4-step process to churn what can be done. The steps in the **DONT** process are:

1. **D**im the focus on what you see and hear around you in the physical world

2. **O**bserve the scene from high above as God sees it

3. **N**arrate the divine scene for your own well-being

4. **T**ell yourself daily what to do as part of your morning meditation

Here is one example we hear, "don't lose your happiness".

Step 1 - Dim your focus on the world around you that makes you lose your happiness. Identify those things you want to dim your focus on? Ex. greed, sorrow, violence, and so on.

Step 2 – Observe the scene through God's ever-loving eyes and feel the happiness it brings. What does God see? Name a few examples of you in your *happy* state, such as 'sweetest, long-lost now found children', students in the Godly University, etc.

Step 3 – Narrate, using your journal, write a description of a scene where all that makes you happy comes to life. Include as many practical examples as you can so a picture forms in your mind.

Step 4 – Tell yourself. Turn your description into a simple commentary that can be repeated to yourself throughout the day to remind you what to do so you 'don't lose your happiness'.

Using this list, select one randomly and work it using the 4-step process. (In a group, put these *don't* statements on slips of paper in a basket - enough for pairs if needed).

- Don't remember the past.

- Don't become disheartened.

- Don't have any desires of this old world.

- Don't perform wrong actions.

- Don't become careless.

- Don't have any desires for wealth.

- Don't think waste thoughts.

- Don't remain asleep.

- Don't remember anyone at the end except the one Father.

Step 1 Dim the focus on the situation by becoming soul conscious. As you contemplate what it looks like when you DO this and what is going on in the world related to this statement. Dim the focus on this scene, and make it blurry, less 'real'.

Step 2 Observe the scene as God sees it with divine vision, if you aren't doing that – what are you doing instead? What are you seeing, hearing, and being? Bring it into focus, make it real.

Step 3 Narrate the scene. In your journal describe what you would be doing, saying, hearing and being.

Step 4 Tell yourself. Put on some quiet instrumental music as background, settle in and read the description of what you have written slowly as a meditation commentary of what God wants you to do. Start with God says 'don't …' and then read your commentary. This is one way of discerning how to best use your energy and sustain the self.

Start the music – enjoy the commentary.

Reflecting on the Experience (Awareness)
- What did you enjoy about this activity?
- How does it help you think about your well-being and health?

Valuing the Art of Sustaining the Self (Attitude)
- What was something in this experiment that you feel will help you sustain your energy, well-being and health?
- What have you discovered is valuable for sustaining the self ~ your energy and your well-being?

Embodying the Art of Sustaining the Self (Action)
- Using discernment, what is something you can start doing to sustain your own health and well-being?
- Repeat your commentary in your morning meditation for one week as a foundation for sustaining the self.

Closing
End with a song.

Resources and References
None.

Living as Art: Harmonizing with Others

*The word 'har' in Hindi means defeat.
Sometimes we must 'bow' to maintain harmony. Although this
can feel like defeat it is achieving victory over one's ego. To
admit to being in the wrong, to accept another's advice or
opinion or to remain silent when unjustly accused are examples
of ego defeat. To 'accept' defeat of ego is to create harmony.*
Inspired by Dadi Janki

Tango is a dance of precision, a practical expression of the art of harmonizing. It is an exquisitely crafted demonstration of respect and cooperation. In tango, there is a subtle 'invitation' to move in one direction and an equally subtle 'response'. Only when an invitation is accepted does the dance proceed. This dance of invitation/response happens quickly but with the full understanding and commitment of each dancer. This makes tango very powerful to watch.

In relationships, there is always a subtle dance of invitation and response. When the energy of cooperation is offered, the dance flows. This dance of cooperation is the art of harmonizing.

The drama of life invites you to offer your cooperation to others. Sometimes you are invited to stand tall and strong, unmoving, so others may lean against your stability. Other times life invites you to bend and flow or to support another as they take the lead.

The art of harmonizing with others is the ability to think in ways that create harmony. It requires an attitude of mutual benefit and invites you to place the quality of relationship as paramount.

This requires an understanding that the only way to maintain your dignity is to honour the dignity of others. Always, even (and especially) when you think they are wrong.

The harmonizing engine of relationships grinds to a halt when the commitment to mutual benefit is missing.

When you hold an attitude and intention of mutual benefit, your perception rises above right/wrong thinking and you discover peaceful pathways forward to maintain harmonious relationships.

If something or someone appears 'wrong' to you, humility allows you to admit that you cannot know the entire back story that created the situation, even when you think you do. This is especially true when you are in it.

Sometimes saying nothing allows the truth to be revealed later in its own time, saving the 'face' of another. This protects a relationship from the righteousness of little ego victories.

> *"Our behaviour towards all should be such that it is full of natural and selfless love, respect, divine family feeling and sweetness. Such a person easily wins over every ones' heart and rules over it. It is said that handsome is that which handsome does."* Br. Jagdish Chandra

Invitation to Contemplate and Write:

- *Remember a time in your family or a group when you felt harmony? What were the elements that created harmony?*
- *What are the virtues needed to sustain harmony in a relationship?*
- *What are the indicators that harmony is present?*
- *What special attention do you need to bring to situations that require a harmony facelift?*
- *How do you keep the energy of benefit flowing in your relationships?*
- *What is your own aim for harmonizing? When? Where? With whom?*

Setting an Intention for Learning: To understand the secrets of harmonizing with others and consider the relevance of these secrets for you.

Meditation

Introducing Harmonizing with Others as Art
Creating harmony is an art when you discover the ways to care for yourself when with others. It involves honouring the dignity of both and generating the energy of mutual benefit. In this way relationships become a dance of invitation/response and life continues smoothly, in harmony.

Experiencing the Art of Harmonizing with Others
To explore the principles of harmony, prepare to listen to the voices of six people (Rajaton from Finland) singing acapella in this song called 'Butterfly'. It is exceptional in its use of harmony. Listen to see if you can detect the principles (rules) of harmony, or in other words, what makes harmony work.

Play Rajaton and jot down notes in your journal about what makes this 6-part harmony work.

Did you notice?
- Sometimes trios sing together, then the trios regroup changing membership each time
- Sometimes all sing in equal volume so it sounds like one blended voice, like velvet
- Sometimes each one sings at a different volume allowing one voice to step forward while the others step back
- Sometimes there are 4 different melodies, each person singing something different

What keeps them on track? There is no conductor, no leader. How do they coordinate their singing? There is a score; each follows their own line on the score.

How much time do you think they spend practicing, to get it right? What percentage alone? What percentage together? In fact, they spend 80% of their time alone, like most musicians, mastering their individual parts. Then they spend 20% of their practice time together.

Harmony is created when each person can keep their attention on their own part, and play it accurately.

How are these principles relevant when you are harmonizing with others? (In group hear comments)

(In a group, try this:
- Identify a common song known in your area – a children's song or a folk song.
- Write down the words.
- Divide into small groups and ask each group to write a new verse of the song using the principles of harmony.
- Then ask each group to prepare to sing their verse in harmony.
- Then sing the whole song with each group singing their verse in harmony. Enjoy and listen for the principles of harmony.)

Reflecting on the Experience (Awareness)
Each of us has a special part to play. We have our own unique note to add.
- Are you singing 'your part' well?
- Check the list of principles for harmony, which do you naturally do?
- Which principles are harder for you?

Valuing the Art of Harmonizing with Others (Attitude)
- What is it about harmonizing that is so important in human relationships?

Embodying the Art of Harmonizing with Others (Action)
- Choose one principle that would help you create harmony with others this week? What virtues will help you with this?

Closing

Play the song *Glorious* by Mormon Children's Choir. Watch YouTube video if possible.

Resources and References
- Song *Butterfly* by Rajaton
- Song *Glorious* by Mormon Children's Choir

Living as Art: Absorbance

Being so full of the positivity I have absorbed in meditation, connected with my highest self and the energy of God, I am able to wash away negativity the way the ocean washes the sand.
Meditation commentary

The soul is like a sponge. It absorbs energy throughout the day. Every situation, every interaction, every thought leaves a trace of energy in the soul. You absorb the energy of your surroundings, the moods of others, their feelings, attitudes and opinions. In addition, when memories play in your mind you become absorbed in energy from a past time. Like a kaleidoscope that keeps changing all day, your inner world is filled with the colors and shapes of the energies you absorb.

**The quality of what is absorbed will either
clean the sponge or clog it.**

The art of absorbance is learning to absorb only that which brings benefit. It means mastering the ability to discern what you allow to influence you and what you choose to *observe* without *absorbing* into yourself. You want to absorb that which is helpful, that which adds energy or uplifts you. And you want to leave aside sorrow and negative energy that brings you down.

As soon as you notice what you are absorbing you have the choice to *observe* and NOT *absorb*. This requires the power to detach from unhelpful energies and focus on the beneficial.

**Absorbance is the capacity of a substance
to absorb light of a specified wavelength.**

Absorbance is the ability to immerse yourself completely in pure, positive energy ~ God's energy or the energy of your highest self. When you are able to concentrate, you can absorb something that is meaningful and not be distracted by the irrelevant. When you hold your mind in a stable thought you can become absorbed in the energy generated by that thought.

"Concentration is the spiritual art of paying full attention on the soul and on God. To not allow the mind to wander in a haphazard manner. When a person has this capacity, they do everything well. Then they become reliable. People say you can give this job to her, as she will do it well. Nothing is sloppy or lazy with concentration." Br. Jagdish Chandra

By mastering this art you can be exposed to the ripple effects of negativity without being affected, just like the ocean absorbs hundreds of rivers. God is a role model in this matter, taking away the mess of confusion and pain inside the soul like blotting paper absorbing a spill ~ yet never being touched by it.

"It was observed in Brahma Baba's life that if any child put his/her confidence in God, God would absorb his weaknesses like an ocean and never express it to others. As such, everyone used to relate his/her mental agony to Brahma Baba with an open mind. Ganesh is shown with a big belly as the symbol of the art of absorbance." Br. Jagdish Chandra

Invitation to Contemplate and Write:

- *Recall a time in meditation when you felt completely absorbed in God's love ~ describe your experience.*
- *What is your capacity to absorb the best and leave the rest?*
- *What happens when you absorb unwanted negativity or sorrow?*
- *How do you protect yourself from absorbing unwanted energies?*
- *How do you discern the quality of energies that surround you daily?*
- *What is your aim in refining the art of absorbance?*

Setting an Intention for Learning: To explore the art of absorbance and maximize your ability to accept high quality energy.

Meditation

Introducing the Art of Absorbance
At a time when advertisers and marketing agencies compete for our attention, we find our minds constantly filled with external messages. Your attention is drawn in many directions at the same time and it becomes difficult to concentrate on one thing. Mind-space or mental attention is a precious commodity and competition is fierce to get it

In this session, we will explore the experience and value of concentrating your awareness to master the art of absorbance.

Experiencing the Art of Absorbance
In preparation for the session, sprout some lentil seeds two days before. (If you have never done it, it's worth the experiment and you get wonderful sprouts to eat afterwards!)

Experiment #1
To begin exploring the art of absorbance, listen to a short audio class by Anthony Strano entitled 'Absorb/Observe.' At the same time, take a handful of dry lentils in one hand and a handful of sprouted ones in the other and contemplate 'how did this hand - with dry lentils turn into that - sprouted lentils?' (In a group give each person a small handful of each.)

Consider:
- What was the process for sprouting? e.g. soaking overnight, daily soak and drain
- Why not leave the seeds in water all the time? E.g. they would drown if in there all the time
- Why is it, when you soak lentils, some sprout and some don't although they have had equal exposure for the same number of days. Some absorbed and some didn't – why? What

enabled some to open to the nourishment of the water, while others could not?
- What would happen to a stone in the same water? Would the same process help the stone to sprout?! (In group, hear comments)

Experiment #2
Take a piece of 'absorbent' paper towel and a pencil. Gently and carefully draw or write something you like on the towel.

With 4 small glasses of colored water, dip a paintbrush into the colored water of your choice and fill in the drawing/writing on the paper towel.
- What happened? What did you notice? Did the water go where you wanted it to go? Could you control what was being absorbed and where it went?

(Hear comments)

Experiment #3
Read this guided commentary, a Raja Yoga meditation which reveals a 4-step process to become absorbed in God's loving energy.

Breathe deeply as you centre yourself in your body...become aware of the sounds around you, the sensation of the chair beneath you and the atmosphere in this room. Now make the choice to draw your thought energy inwards, like a big net extending outwards drawing your attention slowly inwards, bit by bit until it is concentrated in a tiny dot just behind your forehead.

Hold your attention steady on the dot as you become absorbed in the power of your concentrated awareness. Slowly you turn this concentrated awareness upwards and visualize a golden white thread of light extending upwards beyond this room, beyond the sun and moon and stars, beyond the universe to reach the Supreme Light.

Take a moment to greet God with an inner smile and an open heart. Welcome God's loving light to enter your mind and heart and feel this pure energy light you up inside. Imagine your mind filled with light and your heart filled with love. With each physical breath inwards, you receive more of God's love. Another breath and love fills your inner world and you swell with love.

Feel yourself becoming absorbed in this inner experience of love and light. You are radiating light outwards and the vibrations of love now overflow from your mind to the room around you. You are bathed in light. You are bathed in love.

Reflecting on the Experience (Awareness)
- What did you notice about absorbance in these 4 experiments?
- How did you feel watching, listening or feeling absorbance happening in these experiments?

Valuing the Art of Absorbance (Attitude)
- What is the symbolic value of considering the soul to be like the lentil seed or the paper towel, having the capacity to absorb the best vibrations?
- What helps you determine what to absorb and what NOT to absorb?
- What helps you maximize absorbance of positive, powerful vibrations?

Embodying the Art of Absorbance (Action)
- Set an intention for yourself this week to be absorbed in God's loving light in your morning meditation and how you will observe and not absorb negative energies in the world around you.

Closing
Complementary song/music to the art.

Resources and References
- Dry lentils, sprouted lentils – 2 day preparation
- *Absorb-Observe* commentary by Anthony Strano CD *Eight Spiritual Principles of Living.*
- Pencil, paper towel, 4 small jars of water coloured with food colouring, small paint brushes

Living as Art: Being Happy and Content

"One who is happy is also naturally content. Those who are content don't upset others and others don't get upset with them. Who can be truly happy? One with an honest heart. If there is anything else in your heart then you cannot be truly happy."
Dadi Janki

Contentment is an expression of deep satisfaction in the soul. It becomes an art when you understand and practice the thoughts and actions that produce happiness as their fruit.

Contentment is when, at the end of a day, you feel satisfied with yourself ~ when you feel good about what you've done, where you've been and how you've interacted with others. Contentment is feeling grateful for a day well spent.

Behind all your thoughts, words, actions and interactions is a drive to fulfill something...to be satisfied. Discontentment in the soul is an expression of not satisfying this deep drive. Dissatisfaction seeks resolution, often in wrong ways. Then contentment is lost.

Contentment comes from right thinking and right action. It is deeply connected to the conscience. The conscience tells you what is right, if you listen.

It is a secret that the soul is naturally content and needs nothing external to create contentment. In fact, nothing external or material can make the soul content. Only an accurate expression of the self can satisfy the soul. When you are awakened to your inner essence, your actions can be consistent with your deepest self, then you are content.

"Contentment is like an underground river whose course just cannot be daunted. On the surface, people are stamping, pushing, pulling; the ground is cracking or left derelict but underneath, the river is flowing even if at some point, it is only a trickle in the darkness.

Water on ground level is always at risk of pollution or being dried up, used, drunk, drawn on, but subterranean water is untapped. Contentment is the same. It is a constant unseen movement forward. It never dries up.

A profound understanding is needed for someone to be content – a need to know and gently anticipate the movements of the mind, and also, to feel the pull of the destination that lies beyond everything.

To be content, you have to enjoy thinking very deeply, watching every carefully, responding very quietly, moving with the times.

A life lived in contentment can inspire everyone and be possessed by no one, but you. It is yours alone." Anthea Church

Invitation to Contemplate and Write:

- *Remember a time when you experienced deep contentment –what was happening in you? Around you?*
- *In what ways are happiness and contentment like an underground river for you?*
- *How is contentment distinct from being in your 'comfort zone'? How do you discern the difference?*
- *How are happiness and contentment connected for you?*
- *How do you describe your aim for happiness and contentment in life?*

Setting an Intention for Learning: To discover your source of happiness and contentment.

Meditation

Introducing the Art of Being Happy and Content
The art of being happy and content rests on acting like a good businessperson with the things that make you happy and content! Generating a constant supply of happiness is the art, so that the river never goes dry and that you never find yourself scraping the bottom of a dry riverbed in search of a little happiness. To do this you must follow certain spiritual principles – to stay in tune with your true self ~ the soul ~ is to generate happiness. To act out of line with this truth is to create sorrow.

Two pertinent laws of business are:
1. Keep an accurate ledger/account of what comes in and what goes out. Reflect on your day like an accountant – notice when you were happiest today. When did you give happiness to others? When did you cause even slight sorrow for others? Notice what increases your account and what reduces your account of happiness.
2. Analyze your business and set long-term goals. You must know what makes you happy - truly happy, not momentarily happy. To know this is to ensure the maximum measure of happiness in life, and to minimize that which makes you unhappy.

Experiencing the Art of Being Happy and Content
Consider for a few minutes: What makes you happy? List 10 things in your journal that make you happy.

Now review your list and consider business law #2 – what makes you truly happy and content? Select the top 5.

Finally consider: What one item on your list of the top 5 gives you the most happiness? Circle it.

Next, close your eyes and randomly point your finger to one of the happiness quotes below. (In a group setting have each quote on a piece of paper to be selected from a basket - enough for one each)

There is no nourishment like happiness

Never lose your happiness it is your most valuable possession

The more you share and distribute happiness to others, the more your happiness will increase

Happiness follows giving happiness, sorrow follows giving sorrow

Kind and constructive words create a happier world

Consider the quote you have chosen in relation to the #1 thing that makes you happiest. Use the information gathered from this reflection to plan a way to give happiness to someone else. Do something right now that will give happiness to someone else. Use phone, social media.

(In a group, share in pairs - get together by pairs according to duplicate quotes randomly selected from the basket and share what makes you happy. Then use this information to plan a way to give happiness to someone else - another pair in the room.)

Reflecting on the Experience (Awareness)
- What was your experience of giving happiness?
- How did it affect your own level of happiness?

Valuing the Art of Being Happy and Content (Attitude)
- How does giving happiness affect your own level of happiness and contentment?
- What is the value of knowing this equation or spiritual law?

Embodying the Art of Being Happy and Content (Action)
- In what way will you give happiness more…this week and to whom?
- How will you recognize that which gives you happiness?

Closing
Listen to *Happy* by Pharrell Williams

Resources and References
- Music: *Happy* by Pharrel Williams
- Meditation Music: *Piano Lesson* by Andy Blissett on *After the Storm* Available for purchase on-line

Living as Art: Communicating

"When a word is as fragrant as a garden, a conversation is as refreshing as a walk." Anthea Church

Most of us are inundated daily with communication ~ conversations, emails, social media, and advertising. Information flows from so many sources, yet are we really communicating?

Communication is an art when it opens the mind and heart.

Communicating is an art when it is accurate and loveful, then the message, like an arrow, finds its mark. When meaning is concentrated and only that which is needed is spoken, the experience of value is felt in each word. Sometimes just a look and no words are needed.

> *A poet has truly said:*
> *'A sweet word is a medicine and*
> *a bitter word is an arrow;*
> *it affects the entire body*
> *though the hearing path is narrow.'"*
> Br. Jagdish Chandra

Artful communicating involves carefully discerning the essence or core message and conveying it, simply. Indulgence in expansion creates soap opera dramas. Then essence is lost. A return to essence is a rediscovery of meaning.

Expansion is fascinating ~ essence is breathtaking.

"Communication requires sensitivity to simplicity and clarity and the capacity to balance too much/too little. Moments when speech meets action; and both spring out of a single thought into clear expression, are beautiful and rare as gems."
Anthea Church

Feelings are carried through words. A benevolent intention acts as a herald, announcing the arrival of a valuable message. Then the head lifts and ears become alert to receive the precious input. It is the energy inside the message that ensures its delivery is received.

Quiet words spoken with love touch the heart of another, opening it to receive the message. Sweet words soothe. Gentle words guide. Soft words embrace with comfort allowing the other to relax, to settle, to become less prickly.

"There is a saying that the tongue can bestow one with a throne, or can also lead one to the gallows. With sweet words, a person crosses many difficult situations. In soul-consciousness a human always speaks sweet words." Br. Jagdish Chandra

Sometimes the meaning of a message is not easily absorbed. Then patience creates space for the message to be experienced bit by bit until there is recognition of its value. A lightness of spirit makes a 'hard' message easier to hear and a complex idea easier to understand.

"Baba used to entertain and make children laugh while imparting knowledge. He used to clarify several deep secrets of knowledge in a very easy and entertaining manner. He used to cross adverse situations very happily. Baba used to entertain and make children occasionally laugh and would say, "Always keep on smiling like flowers." Br. Jagdish Chandra

The crux of communication is wastage. When you say too much, the core meaning can be lost. It is an art to discover the core message and convey it well. In our spiritual practice, we strive to be essence-full, to get to the point. To do this, we must become a point (become soul conscious) and put a full stop to waste thoughts. The simpler and more pure we become, the less energy we waste attempting to communicate.

"Now put a full stop to all confusion, reaction and expansion from the past. A full stop is a point. When you do not put a full-stop, that is when you do not stabilize yourself in the point form,

you either put an exclamation mark, a comma or a question mark. This is also the basis for the creation of waste thoughts. Whatever happens, continue to observe it as a detached observer, a dot." Avyakt BapDada

Invitation to Contemplate and Write:

- *Remember a time when you really appreciated the way a difficult message was communicated to you ~ what was the nature of the delivery?*
- *Think of a time when you chose very carefully what you would say to someone ~ what influenced your wish to be careful?*
- *What was the sweetest message you ever received? What made it sweet?*
- *How can you discern the accuracy of a message?*
- *How do you know the difference between essence and expansion?*
- *What is an aim you have for your own communication?*

Setting an Intention for Learning: To experiment with communicating as a fine art.

Meditation

Introducing the Art of Communicating
The art of communicating involves knowing what you want to express then conveying it simply with pure intention and no waste. When the feeling matches the message, the vibration is understood even if the words are not.

For this you must learn to manage your own waste ~ that which leads you into expansion or side scenes.

> *"One does not accumulate but eliminate. It is not daily increase but daily decrease that matters. The height of cultivation always runs to simplicity."* Bruce Lee

Experiencing the Art of Communicating
'The period' (another punctuation mark) was recently declared dead! (Adbusters, 2017 the Death of the period).

Part of our *spiritual effort now is to put a full stop,* to use the period to move into essence.

Consider the consciousness behind each of the following punctuation marks: the comma, the exclamation mark and the question mark.

Place each punctuation mark on a piece of paper and write your thoughts underneath. (In a group use a flipchart and gather input for each punctuation mark.)
- ! What is the consciousness behind the use of exclamation marks in communicating? Write ideas.
- ? What is the consciousness behind the use of question marks in communicating? Write ideas.
- , What is in someone's consciousness when commas are used a lot when communicating?

Write ideas. (In a group, hear comments and write on flipchart)

Look at the list below and spend 3 minutes considering which of these punctuation marks best describes your communication style? And what is the reason behind this specific choice?

! ? ,

- Splat energy across the space
- Forceful energy in your face
- Exaggeration
- Extra emphasis to make an impression

What makes you exaggerate or over- emphasize or be reactive?

- Wandering complexity
- Doubt
- Confusion
- Twist in knots
- lack clarity
- lack self-confidence or self-respect

What twists you into confusion or doubt?

- *"That'll do comma"*
- Run on sentences
- Expansion
- Add another thought then another …
- 17 rules for commas - most overused punctuation mark

When, how do you extend yourself and continue to speak expansively?

Reflecting on the Experience (Awareness)
- What are you more aware of in relation to communicating?

Valuing the Art of Communicating (Attitude)
- What do you consider an important quality to be expressed through your communication? (hear group comments)

Embodying the Art of Communicating (Action)
- Consider an action you might take this week to refine communicating as an art. Sum it up in a diamond poem as shown in the sample below (9 words in the shape of a diamond.)

A
poem that
creates a diamond
like shape
!

Read out loud. (Everyone in a group.)

Closing
Complementary song/music to the art.

Resources and References
- Hand-out: The Art of Communicating
- Music

Living as Art: Leading

"Harbour a flawless quality inside of you, preserve it, nurture it and use it at the time it is most needed. Then it is the quality that leads, not you." Anthea Church

Leading is an art when ego is removed and the qualities required in a situation are brought forth to lead. The art of leading is about creating an atmosphere where the best qualities in everyone emerge. Then the collective will creates a beautiful dance of leading and following.

To make others into leaders is the sign of a great leader.

Leadership is personal ~ it begins with self-mastery. As each person learns to master themselves (their reactions and habits), there is little need for a designated leader to get the job done.

Leadership is about working with qualities. Leading encourages the discovery and full expression of each person's innate qualities thus directing these qualities towards the task at hand.

An accurate assessment of each situation enables you to recognize the qualities needed and available. Then you adjust yourself to the need, sometimes stepping back, sometimes coming closer or encouraging patiently. When the qualities of each one in the group are seen and honoured, they grow and become a significant contribution.

The art of leading is about discovering the qualities in you that help others be and give their best.

The art of leading is based on your ability to be a good follower. To follow the highest standard of human conduct is to stay true to that which is beneficial for everyone. Following your conscience, following your highest values in all situations makes you a role model. Then you automatically lead because others look to you for insight, integrity and guidance. By opening pathways for others to thrive and shine, a leader wins blessings and loyalty. People trust leadership that is honest, selfless and values-based.

> *"The leader's task is to awaken people to their own greatness ~ to encourage people to progress, to turn every effort maker into a leader or a teacher. Brahma Baba engaged everyone in active service as per his/her qualities so that each might develop their potentiality."* Br. Jagdish Chandra

Leading is also about using resources wisely. In organization and management settings, leadership is concerned with the best use of things - time, personnel, equipment, supplies, money, buildings, etc.

On the spiritual journey, you learn to make the best use of your inherent qualities. As a soul, you have buried inside you a storehouse of five original qualities – *Peace, Purity, Wisdom, Love and Happiness/Bliss*. The art of leading involves being aware of these qualities and using them in a worthwhile way for the betterment of humanity and the world.

Invitation to Contemplate and Write:

- *Think of a time in a group when you experienced the exhilaration of doing something that benefitted many people? What were the qualities and contributions of leadership that shone? What was your role?*
- *When is leadership needed? What does it look like at its best?*
- *What are the highest principles that guide leadership?*
- *What is your code of conduct for leadership?*
- *What is the best use of your innate qualities in activities you carry out with others?*
- *What is your aim for developing your own leadership?*

Setting an Intention for Learning: To explore qualities that refine the art of leading.

Meditation

Introducing the Art of Leading
Leadership looks for and expects high quality (calibre) contributions from people. Often, leaders are frustrated due to low quality input and use threats or incentives to motivate people to give more.

However, the art of leading is about working with qualities ~ to be in tune with the qualities required to get a job done. Leadership seeks out the highest qualities and potential in everyone and nurtures them. When people are supported to express their best, a task becomes easy and everyone follows the pathway of cooperation.

Experiencing the Art of Leading
Experiment #1
Recall a time in a group when you experienced the exhilaration of doing something that benefitted many people? Jot down notes in your journal. (Hear comments in a group)

Collect an array of objects that are different from each other (8 is enough for yourself and more are needed for a group. Find daily objects cup, scissors, stuffed toy, basket, notebook, calculator, flower, candle, music instrument, etc.) and place them randomly on a table in front of you.

Take a moment and then choose an object. (Ask group members to select.)

After choosing, reflect on what quality or virtue led you to choose the object you selected? Use your journal to capture some of the qualities/virtues that come to your mind. (Hear from each person in the group.)

Read the following passage and make note of your response.

"Leadership, as an art is not to do with being in charge of people, it is to do with command of quality. When there is inside you a flawless quality, something that has been preserved or nurtured, in the instant when that quality is needed, you become a leader. Not you, but it, because it springs from your depths, it projects deep into situations; it reaches the heart and changes it. Quality is the leader. Problems only come when people lead. Where only quality leads, there is no name, there is no figurehead – there is just a resource." Anthea Church

(Hear group responses.)

Experiment #2
Now take a moment and identify a quality (virtue) you would like to take the lead more in your life.

Stand up and let that quality physically lead you in a silent walk for the next 5 minutes - move around the space where you are holding the awareness of the quality you have chosen, in silence, allowing this quality to lead you. Follow it.

Sit down after 5 minutes and reflect on this experience of letting a quality lead – what did it feel like, what was different from how you have led or been led in the past? Jot down notes in your journal. (Hear comments in the group after some reflection time.)

Experiment #3
Print the innate qualities or resources of the soul (*peace, purity, love, wisdom, happiness*) on blue paper and senses (*seeing, hearing, tasting, feeling, and smelling*) on another coloured paper. Cut in strips to use later.

You have 5 physical senses through which to express these five qualities in the world – seeing, hearing, tasting, feeling, and smelling. One aspect of the art of leading is to manage or administer all resources well. Here are some helpful examples of how the senses express the inherent qualities in the world.

- *The sense of listening makes the quality of love visible – ex. I will give my full attention to the one in front of me, when they speak I listen with my eyes, ears, heart.*

- *The sense of taste manifests the quality of peace – ex. I take my tea break in silence and be thankful for each mouthful used to sustain and maintain my energy for the task ahead.*

Here you will develop your own meditation to use the senses to effectively and efficiently display the 5 original qualities in your workplace. Pick one slip of blue paper, a quality; and a slip of yellow paper, a sense on it.

In meditation, go inward and connect with that leadership quality, then go upward to the Supreme Source of abundance of that quality and allow images to flow for how you could use the chosen sense to exhibit that quality in your life. Say it aloud, record it. Repeat picking up a different quality and matching it with a sense. Once you have recorded all five, put on soft music and settle into a meditation to lead yourself using your inner qualities.

(In a group, put on low meditation music, the facilitator will start and share how to use that sense to express that leadership quality. She then touches the person next to her, who waits a few minutes and then shares his given quality and how to express leadership using it. He then touches the next person, who waits and then shares. Go around the group until each one in turn has shared in the collective commentary.)

Reflecting on the Experience (Awareness)
- What are you aware of when a quality or virtue leads? How did it feel or look different from previous experiences of leadership?
- What did you notice in the meditation about the senses and how they could be used to express the qualities?

Valuing the Art of Leading (Attitude)
- What is valuable about the approach of letting qualities lead? How does this compare to having a person lead?
- What is important about how you employ these qualities with your physical senses to enhance leadership? (hear comments)

Embodying the Art of Leading (Action)
- Choose a card from the self-mastery deck and make a schedule for when and where you will let this virtue/quality lead this week. Make notes in your journal to reflect on your experience of leading in this way – include both your own reactions and those of others.

Closing
Complementary song/music to the art.

Resources and References
- Deck of self-mastery cards (If you do not have access to a set of self-mastery cards, please see a list of virtues in the resource section.)

Living as Art: Learning and Teaching

"Learning implies transformation in one's life. Brahma Baba, even after attaining old age, always used to consider himself just a student. This attitude took him to the peak of the heights. Learning needs inquisitiveness." Br. Jagdish Chandra

To be a skilled learner is essential to the art of teaching. Teaching the self well is the art of learning.

Learning and teaching; both must travel hand in hand for the journey to be balanced and for wisdom to be distilled. When learning leads, both teacher and learner follow pathways of inquiry rather than following rote methods, blind faith or other people.

Both learning and teaching require mastering the ability to feel the pulse of interest and motivation of the learner and create a bridge to the subject to be learned.

Standing in the awareness of what is ready to open inside, the learner seeks out the teacher(s) who will guide its expression. In this way teaching and learning are drawn together.

The teacher appears when the learner is ready.

When you are the teacher, you learn to discern the interests, needs and strengths of the learner. When you are the learner, you teach by sharing your insights and interests. It is a dance that requires two.

Effective teaching comes from the experience of constant learning. An attitude of openness and genuine curiosity are prerequisites for learning and teaching. A wise teacher frames a question that inspires deeper investigation and draws both learner and teacher onto the learning journey, as companions.

"Although there are four subjects in Raja Yoga, Brahma Baba used to teach it in such a way as if he was teaching a single subject and was teaching the same like a story. There used to be intimacy between the teacher and the student.

The essence of the art of teaching is loveful behavior. Brahma Baba ~ with his sweet actions, loving spiritual vision, positive attitude and behaviour ~ used to teach the children the lesson of belongingness. Saint Kabir Das has said this in his meaningful words, 'Studying books after books, the world has passed by, none has become really knowledgeable. One who learns one short word ~ love ~ becomes truly knowledgeable.'"
Br. Jagdish Chandra

A learner yearns for the satisfaction of meaning-making. The teacher shares this quest, and together they explore the meaning of lived experiences and the scenes around them. A shared love for learning leads the way to new discoveries.

The best teaching is based on the authority of experience. In a world where the ruling paradigm privileges hierarchy and position, the power of personal experience can be lost. When learning leads the way, inquiry facilitates the learner's discovery of their own innate wisdom.

Learning and teaching ignite conversations that open hearts and minds to the healing vibrations of wonder. New possibilities become public. New behaviours result. Together they create a new world.

Invitation to Contemplate and Write:

- *Remember a time when you learned something new ~ what feelings do you associate with that experience?*
- *What motivates you to learn? What motivates you to teach?*
- *How do you know when to tell and when to ask?*
- *How can you both learn and teach at the same time?*
- *What is your aim for developing your 'teaching and learning'?*

Setting an Intention for Learning: To explore the spiritual aspects of learning and teaching.

Meditation

Introducing the Art of Learning and Teaching
Learning and teaching are about gaining greater levels of awareness, making attitudinal shifts that work and acquiring new skills, as in these sessions.

Awareness is about knowing ~ it is spirit, it is alive. You have a responsibility to use your new awareness, attitudes and skills to transform yourself and to pass it on to others. Knowledge cannot belong to anyone, it is not yours nor can you own it. You are a conduit/an instrument for knowledge to pass through.

> **Wisdom is our collective knowing.**

There is so much to know, especially in Raja Yoga. There is so much to learn about soul consciousness. Just the one thought "I am a soul" is filled with much to learn about how to be in the point form. Then, in yoga, learning to connect with God and being open to new relationships with the Divine.

Experiencing the Art of Learning and Teaching
In this session, you will explore experiences with learning and teaching by experiencing *a variety of postures for meditation*. Each posture has a different purpose and benefit. You will experiment with meditations about learning and teaching while walking, standing, lying and sitting. You will give about 5 minutes to each posture. This is called the *Wisdom Tree meditation.*

Start in a lying position - we'll move through each meditation and finish up in the seated position.

Posture #1
Lie down, stretch out, and keep your eyes open as you begin your meditation. The lying meditation pose is about healing and forgiveness. Breathe deeply. Imagine a tall tree in front of you

with many wide strong branches extending from its trunk reaching up towards the sky. Imagine yourself lying safely on the first branch of the tree with a member of your birth family. This is about love and innocence.
- Who is the other? Who is teaching? Who is learning?
- What happens between the two that takes you beyond what is already known?

Posture #2
Now stand up and in full meditative awareness, for a standing meditation and connect with the full power of the self. Imagine yourself moving up to the next large branch where you stand with a member of your extended family of friends and colleagues with love and honesty.
- Who is the other? Who is teaching? Who is learning?
- What happens between the two that takes you beyond what is already known?

Posture #3
Now move into a walking meditation which is about innovation and creativity. Imagine you move up to a higher strong branch of this mighty Tree of Wisdom and you find yourself walking with an historical figure with love and truth.
- Who is the other? Who is teaching? Who is learning?
- What happens between the two that takes you beyond what is already known?

Posture #4
Now sit down in full meditative awareness in this waiting and listening pose. Imagine you are on one of the highest branches of the strong and sturdy wisdom tree. Sitting with you is your spiritual guide.
- Who is the other? Who is teaching? Who is learning?
- What happens between the two that takes you beyond what is already known?

Reflecting on the Experience (Awareness)
Gently bring all these images of the tree of wisdom back with you and sit with your journal and reflect on your experiences on the wisdom tree.
- When you were teaching, what did you notice about the learning process?
- When you were learning, what did you notice about the teaching process?
- When you were the one helping someone else to learn, what did you discover about your own learning process?
  (In a group, ask people to share highlights from their reflections)

Valuing the Art of Learning and Teaching (Attitude)
- What virtues bring learning and teaching together? At what moments do the same virtues need to be present in both?
- What do you value most about the contribution that teaching and learning can make to living life as art?

Embodying the Art of Learning and Teaching (Action)
- Choose one insight about the art of learning and teaching that you will put into practice this week - wrap this in loving light and carry it with you as a determined thought for yourself as learner and teacher this week.

Closing
Complementary song/music to the art.

Resources and References
None.

Living as Art: Revealing and Concealing

"Life reveals its secrets to us. But not often before its' time, before it's ready. And sometimes we may wish to share something but it's not time for it to be seen or heard so no one listens. Even if you wished to, you couldn't speak a secret before its time for if you did, no one would hear it." Anthea Church

It is an art to know when to keep something to yourself and when to share. There are moments when it's appropriate and beneficial to share. Other moments it is best to remain quiet and wait. The art of revealing and concealing requires mastery of the subtle aspects of timing, discretion and maturity.

There are times when revealing information is beneficial because it serves to:
- shed light on a shared understanding and support the creation of unity
- offer insight into a situation so an individual can adjust or take action accordingly
- engage and include the input of others thus opening the doors for co-creation
- invite others to see and be uplifted by the revealed truth

Not sharing in such moments could add to an atmosphere of mistrust, disunity or disharmony.

However, something newsworthy can provoke excitement to share. This is a signal that ego is urging sharing, to make you 'the one' who knows and has the power to include others in the club of 'those-who-know'. Mastery in the art of revealing and concealing prevents secrets from becoming a currency of power and a basis for creating subtle alliances which unleash politics, breed familiarity and indulge in unhelpful expansion.

"Seek perfection in private." Anthea Church

There are times when concealing information is beneficial because it serves to:
- protect a situation or person from premature discovery and possible meddling or interventions that could threaten natural development
- allow time and space for reflection and perceptions to shift naturally

Wisdom allows you to discern subtle insecurities that fester around a piece of "news" that, if shared, could ignite misunderstanding or hurt feelings. Revealing prematurely at these times would create an atmosphere of insecurity or pressure. Sometimes it is best to grow alone.

Invitation to Contemplate and Write:

- *Recall a time when you accurately assessed the signals for what to reveal and what to conceal. What was happening in you that helped you discern?*
- *When have you been the recipient of "don't tell a soul" news? How did you feel? What was the benefit to the person sharing?*
- *When have you been uncomfortable receiving or sharing news/information? Why?*
- *What is your aim regarding mastering the art of revealing and concealing?*

Setting an Intention for Learning: To explore how the art of revealing and concealing can contribute to my spiritual growth.

Preparation: In the week preceding this session, take a piece of paper and each day of the week, write a beautiful, meditative line and fold it over so it can't be seen the next day. Continue for 5-6 days.

Meditation

Introducing the Art of Revealing and Concealing
It is an art to know when to keep something to yourself and when to share it. There are moments when it's appropriate and beneficial to share. Other moments it is best to remain quiet and wait. The art of revealing and concealing requires mastery of the subtle aspects of timing, discretion and maturity.

Experiencing the Art of Revealing and Concealing
Here are a series of experiments for you to use to explore this art.

Experiment #1
Put on some quiet music, take the paper with the beautiful meditative lines written on it, unfold it and read as a commentary.

Consider what that experience was like? How did time and concealing a line daily contribute to your experience?

Experiment #2
Consider the kind of person with whom you could share the secrets of your heart, knowing they are safe, that they will never be shared or even spoken of unless you raise them again yourself. Be aware as you write that such discretion and respect is hard to find.

Write in your journal about what such a person is like.

Next consider the kind of person with whom you cannot share the secrets of your heart for you know they will tell others and

your vulnerability will be revealed or they will bring up your vulnerabilities again later in an unsafe context.
Describe that kind of person in your journal.

Reflect for a moment:
- What does knowing these two kinds of people suggest to you about revealing and concealing?

Experiment #3
Consider this diagram based on the **Ring Theory** *by Susan Silk and Barry Goldman*

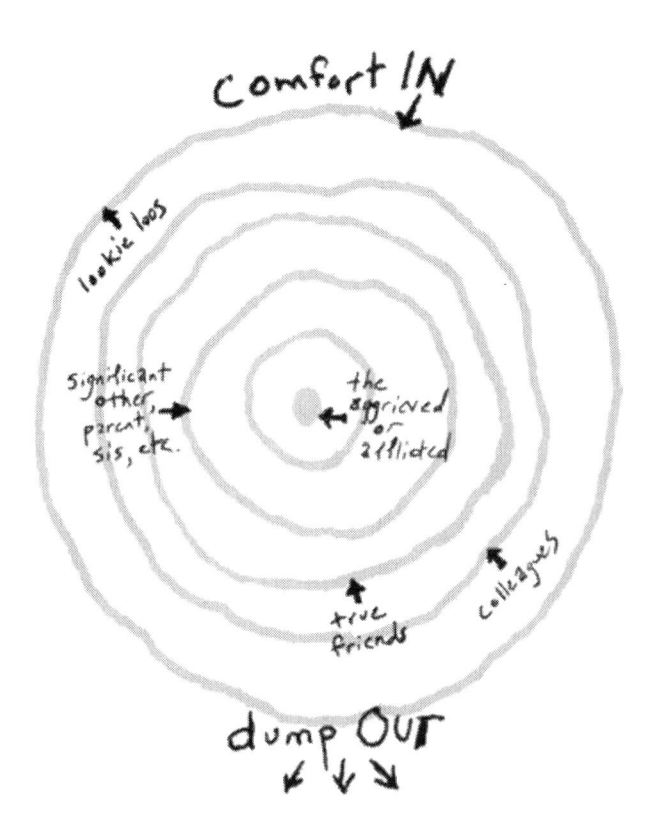

[Diagram: concentric rings labeled from center outward: "the aggrieved or afflicted" (center), "significant other, parent, sis, etc.", "true friends", "colleagues", "lookie loos". Arrows indicate "comfort IN" (pointing inward) and "dump OUT" (pointing outward).]

The creators of this diagram suggest a simple principle: the person most directly affected by a challenging situation has the choice to dump out - meaning to share their feelings, difficulties and complaints about the hard time outwards to any other level of the circle.

However, a person further removed from the direct effect of the situation should NOT dump their thoughts, feelings or opinions inward to the next level of people affected, but CAN, however, dump outwards to someone who is less directly involved in the situation. And they should offer COMFORT to the inner rings where people are being more directly affected by the situation.

The rule of thumb is: **DUMP OUT, COMFORT IN.**

Make two lists of wise criteria to apply when discerning whether to reveal or conceal – one for when to reveal and one for when to conceal.

Consider:
- What is at stake when you are deciding whether to reveal or conceal? What are your guidelines?
- What kinds of situations require this art?
- Draw your own ring diagram placing yourself and a challenging situation at the centre OR someone in your life and their situation.

Experiment #4
Take a piece of white paper and crumple it forcefully in your hand. Now open the paper and smooth it out completely. What do you notice? Ex. that can't undo what is done but we can learn from it.

Experiment #5
Sit with your journal and for 8 minutes put pen to paper and without lifting your pen, write a story about a *secret that you have learned from life*.

Consider what you wrote and the way you learned this secret.
- How was this secret been revealed to you? In other words, how did life teach you this secret? or how did you learn this secret from life?

Experiment #6
Watch this video #CreateCourage - Rogue One: A Star Wars Story

Reflecting on the Experience (Awareness)
- What did you notice about revealing and concealing from the experiments during this session? What was new for you in this session?

Valuing the Art of Revealing and Concealing (Attitude)
- What do these activities suggest to you about the art of revealing and concealing?
- What is something very significant for you to remember about revealing and concealing from this session?

Embodying the Art of Revealing and Concealing (Action)
- What is the wisdom you will bring to discerning accurately whether and when to reveal/conceal this week?

Closing (complementary song/music to the art)

Resources and References
- Paper with meditative writing from previous week
- YouTube Video: *#CreateCourage Rogue One: A Star Wars Story*
- Article *Ring Theory* by Susan Silk and Barry Goldman in www.latimes.com

Living as Art: Moving Forward

"Our goal in life should always be elevated and we should go on making efforts to attain that goal. Whatever challenges (tests) come on the way, always go on marching ahead. Then our progress would become a source of inspiration for others too."
Br. Jagdish Chandra

Skipping along with enthusiasm, the child steps lightly and happily on each stepping stone of the journey. Slight alterations in the path are considered with delight, a game to be chased to its conclusion. Stubbing a toe along the way breaks momentum but only momentarily. Perhaps a period of sitting on the side offers the promise of refreshment…then we're off again.

However, if there is a distraction during this temporary break, friends can move along and you can be left behind, absorbed in the novelty of something new. It is possible that a break from movement seduces the skipping child to stop, to become distracted and forget the original direction entirely.

When a distraction becomes the destination, momentum is lost.

When distracted, you can find yourself wandering off the main path, yet somehow with the illusion of progressing.

It is an art to notice the side scenes, to take a break when needed and always to carry on. This requires a love for journeying and a total focus on the destination. Then even when the body is tired the mind will invent new ways to keep skipping.

Sometimes stopping provides an opportunity to catch a breath, take a rest and confirm movement in the same direction with renewed enthusiasm. At other times a diversion or obstacle is a signal to stop and reconsider your approach or possibly a new direction altogether. But there are times when stopping for a diversion draws you into stagnation and a loss of direction.

When the destination is an expression of a golden intention, it is easy to keep it in your mind and heart.

The Art of Moving Forward is the ability to continue ~ always, learning to balance and pace rests with reflection while never losing focus or enthusiasm for the ultimate destination.

Br. Jagdish spoke extensively about the art of moving forward. Here are three aspects he highlighted:

"As well as the ability to stop we must also be able to start doing something. I must be able to move myself and make others move. To move and to make others move. We have to learn both. Some people know how to move themselves, but cannot move others. Those who have the ability to make others move are leaders.

I have to make my mind move on the positive path of thinking. Stop the negative thinking and move it towards the positive thinking. This is what yoga or spiritual consciousness is. Previously we were aware of the body. Now we think we are souls, children of God and these positive thoughts fill my mind. This is called a pilgrimage of remembrance. Why a pilgrimage? Why not remembrance only? Because we must move towards our home, to move from body consciousness to subtle consciousness. This kind of movement has to be taken now.

Also churning is moving the mind, cogitating and integrating what you have listened to. We must engage our minds in churning spiritual knowledge. Sometimes we have to move fast. Anyone who makes sincere spiritual effort is a fast effort maker. When the airplane is at the airport, it first stands still, then it begins to move, then it moves very fast. Before going into the air, it goes very fast. Similarly, we can attain the flying stage when we move fast. When we stop old negative thoughts, and move our minds into churning and positive thinking we move fast with rapid speed and then become angels." Br. Jagdish Chandra

Invitation to Contemplate and Write:

- *Recall a time when you recognized you were making progress on your spiritual journey ~ what was the experience? How did you know you were making progress?*
- *What are some distractions or obstacles on your spiritual journey?*
- *Sometimes obstacles or diversions act as **stepping** stones and sometimes they act as **stopping** stones. How do you know the difference?*
- *What are some successful ways you get through or around these distractions or obstacles?*
- *What is the aim/destination for your own spiritual journey?*
- *What are 3 indicators that you are making progress? What 3 signs would indicate to you that you are moving forward on your spiritual journey?*

Setting an Intention for Learning: To explore what it takes to keep moving forward in my spiritual life.

Meditation

Introducing the Art of Moving Forward
The Art of Moving Forward is the ability to continue, always. Over time, as the journey of life continues, one gets tired. When fatigued, it is possible to lose sight of the destination or to lose enthusiasm for the journey itself. Then side scenes demand attention and draw further energy away from the main path.

The spiritual journey (and life) is a marathon not a sprint, there are times to move fast and times to rest and reflect. In a society where action is everything, it is important to learn the art of pacing. And to discover the secrets of what keeps you going.

The Art of Moving Forward is learning to balance rest and reflection with forward movement to continue without getting tired. It means to always keep sight of, and enthusiasm for, the ultimate destination.

Experiencing the Art of Moving Forward
Stand up and chose a point across the room – then count the number of steps it takes as you march across the room to that point. You have arrived ... somewhere!

Now from this spot choose another spot across the room and go there - using the same number of steps to get there. When you arrive, or run into obstacles, or run out of time, or run out of steps, stop and reflect on what happened.

Take out for journal and consider:
- Did you reach your destination or did you miss it?
- What helped you move forward on your journey?
- What impeded your progress on your journey? How did you address it? (in group hear comments)

Now do it one more time, look across the room, pick a spot and head there using the same number of steps.
- What happened this time - did you make it or miss it?
- What helped or got in the way this time?
- What did you notice about your reactions to each of the 3 journeys?
- How does this mimic life's journey? What can you learn from this? (hear comments)

Reflecting on the Experience (Awareness)
- What does this activity suggest to you about moving forward on your spiritual path?
- What was surprising or challenging for you on the journeys? (hear comments)

Valuing the Art of Moving Forward (Attitude)
- What is an important insight about these symbolic journeys for you to apply on your spiritual journey? (hear comments)

Embodying the Art of Moving Forward (Action)
- What is one intention or practice you would like to maintain on your spiritual journey?
- What is one obstacle that might stop you in your progress? How will you address this challenge in a way that allows you to keep moving forward?
- What is one thing you will do each day to keep moving forward on your spiritual journey? (hear comments)

Closing
Complementary song/music to the art.

Resources and References
- Song *Sign of a Victory* by R. Kelly

Living as Art: Serving

"Let every act of serving benefit both the other and the self."
Avyakt BapDada

The desire to give is a natural expression of love. Love is the core energy of the soul. In a world of business transactions, where give and take is the law of the land, this spiritual art conquers the ego of keeping a balance sheet in relationships. It means setting ego aside so God's pure energy can guide the giving.

Ego demands an outcome. God gives. God encourages you to offer consistently high quality input without expectation of return.

Ego demands to be seen and appreciated for giving. God remains incognito and guides you to give quietly as a natural expression of who you are, without seeking attention or praise. God says: 'Sweet child, you may not be well known to the world but you are well known to me.'

The art of serving is to both give and receive at the same time.

In order to have anything to give, you must be receiving something or you will be depleted. When you give your mind and intellect for God to use as needed, then you receive God's pure energy which sustains you. And there is no need to take from others.

When you give God your honest heart, you receive the pure, spiritual energy from God that dissolves your weaknesses. When you receive in this way, you are filled with such love and strength that it overflows and is naturally shared with others. If tuned in and receiving from God you always have something to give. Then it's all about your capacity to receive because it determines how much you can give.

When you are receiving and full you are able to discern what will bring the greatest benefit in any situation. You will know what to give to uplift others.

When you are full it is easier to give space so others may step forward. This means to receive a rest break.

The art of giving and receiving is like being the glove and allowing God's energy to be the hand that moves you to say and do only that which brings benefit, even if you never see it. The results are known only by the one who receives help. And by God, of course.

When the giver is invisible, the experience of receiving or being helped comes free of charge. There is no feeling of a price tag attached, not even of expecting a thank you. Because there are no strings attached and no return expected, there is no disappointment, resentment, fatigue or bondage. You remain tireless, light, happy and free.

"It's a big thing to be a real server of people, and yet done to the utmost, it nourishes the heart of you, for in 'utterness' you are touching with your heart the seed of the matter, and so it is the heart of you that feels the return.

When the heart is used, there is a radiation outwards and what is reached is not the heads of people with the power to change THINGS, but their hearts – and then they change themselves...and physical things follow in the wake.

You don't need any resources to serve from the heart, but you need to be rich inside. Rich means you've got space and space means an open heart. To serve from your heart is to give yourself to life. Not your words, or your energy or your busy-ness, but yourself.

With heart, you can just think, and things begin to happen. In thought, you go straight to the heart. Like an arrow, a thought sent is sent. When there is virtue in the thought, the arrow touches the heart. Virtue puts its arm around a person and offers what is needed in that moment. How do we learn to serve in this way?" Anthea Church

Invitation to Contemplate and Write:

- *Recall a time when something you offered made a great difference spiritually for many others. What did the service look like? Feel like?*
- *How is spiritual service different than any other kind of service?*
- *What does it mean to be a world server?*
- *How do you integrate giving and receiving so you are never tired, nor ever expect a return (of praise or appreciation or seeing results)?*
- *What are you receiving from God in this moment?*
- *What is your aim as you come to understand true service?*

Setting an Intention for Learning: To explore serving as a spiritual art.

Meditation

Introducing the Art of Serving
We have been given the treasures of spiritual knowledge, virtues, and powers through our study of Raja Yoga. These are our riches – they are to use in practical daily life and for the service of humanity.

When you look at someone with the awareness that they are a soul, you begin to 'see' their subtle qualities and virtues. Then the other person will experience them as well. They will become aware of their own qualities and be able to use them when needed. This becomes a blessing for the soul. As a server, this requires the practice of soul consciousness.

> *"In the moment of weakness, a soul cannot imbibe knowledge (make sense or understand something). In that moment they need power. With feelings of mercy and compassion, with the help of all your powers and virtues you must help to uplift them: this is a form of blessing."* Avyakt BapDada

Experiencing the Art of Serving
There are many ways to serve. Let's generate a list - charity, donations of physical goods, giving of time to help in tasks, fighting battles for/with someone or on their behalf. Take out your journal and ask what are other ways to serve? (Ask a group to consider in silence then share.)

Consider which of these has a spiritual aspect? What makes it spiritual?

Experiment #1
Now take a moment to reflect on a time when you really ***needed*** help – consider what kind of help was needed? It may have been recently or long ago, it may have been physical, emotional, social or spiritual help or some combination. Reflect silently for

a moment. Then remember a time when you *received* the help you needed – recall how it felt?

Then read these statements below and recall if they were part of your experience.

- *the feeling of someone else's thoughts changing something inside you*

- *the feeling of support as you looked in someone's face and saw not their features, but that support touching you*

- *the feeling of being light, of being like a child again in spirit and feeling the burden lifted from you*

- *the feeling of tirelessness, when you had been through something and felt fatigue, with traces of the journey still on your face, yet the heaviness was absorbed for you so that you could celebrate the accomplishment without fatigue*

Write in your journal about this experience. Tell it as a story about receiving true service. Automatic write for 10 minutes. (This means writing without lifting your pen from the paper, to let the subconscious mind speak without editing.)

(In a group - Share stories with trios – tell about the experience of receiving true service)

Experiment #2
Stabilize yourself in soul consciousness … and look in the mirror and see the one reflected back to you as soul. Have no intention other than to see this soul – in the awareness of yourself as soul – no intention to give. Stay open to being an instrument through which God's energy can flow. That's all. Have one full minute – stabilize in the awareness of yourself as a soul, notice fluctuation, it's okay, come back to soul consciousness.

(In groups, invite people to practice – divide the group in half, create an inner circle facing outward and outer circle standing in front of each one in the inner circle. After a minute those in the outer circle will move one to the left and repeat the soul conscious experience (also known as drishti) and so on around the circle. Use a quiet chime to announce when the minute is up. When the drishti circle is complete - close your eyes, notice how you are feeling and hold that feeling in your awareness as you leave the circle).

Reflecting on the Experience (Awareness)
- What was inspiring in your story about serving? Surprising?
- From this story, what do you understand about the nature of true service? (In a group setting – hear comments and what are some commonalties or similarities among the stories of true service shared?)
- What was the experience like of giving and receiving pure soul conscious vision to/from yourself? (to/from others?)

Valuing the Art of Serving (Attitude)
- Thinking about someone or some situation in your life right now, where could true service be of great value to you and others? (Hear samples if in group)

Embodying the Art of Serving (Action)
- How will you put the insights about spiritual serving into practice this week for the benefit of all?

Closing
Song *Lifted* by Bliss

Resources and References
- Song *Lifted* by Bliss
- Mirror, journal

Living as Art: Transformation

Surrendering to your highest potential is the key to unlock the transformative process. Without knowing all the details of the end state, even a small taste of its beauty ignites the will to transform.

Transforming becomes an art when you see the newness inside of you that is ready to emerge and you understand the balance of creation and destruction required to let it grow.

Sustaining is the secret to transformation.

When you love and honour a small, pure beginning, you are able to nurture and sustain it long enough for it to flourish. Keeping a protective eye on the silent emerging self allows it to grow naturally in its own time. Transformation occurs during this 'in-between' phase. Patience is paramount.

"Baba used to say that after understanding one's duty and aim of life, it was not difficult to mould oneself and transform one's life style and old habits. In Brahma Baba's own life, such transformation was evident. From the day he experienced his first vision the transformation started taking place. 'Quick effort means quick transformation', Baba adopted this technique in his life as a great formula." Br. Jagdish Chandra

Befriending your highest potential enables you to shed the tight costume of old beliefs and habits that restrain its emergence. Although you have invested vast energies in the construction and accumulation of the current architecture called 'I/me/myself', in your heart you long to return to the simple, sincere sweetness of your natural state. This longing intensifies the closer you get to it.

Paying careful attention to the growth of your potential allows you to detect the small indicators of its development. Seeing and feeling this subtle evidence gives courage to continue the transformative journey.

> *"People convert waste iron or gold into new articles by melting. Similarly, after making others give up their old habits, Baba used to inspire them to transform these into good habits. He always upheld the pious thought to transform the vicious world into a viceless world."* Br. Jagdish Chandra

Creation begins in the mind. Thought is the seed of all newness. When your perceptions are fixed, you are unable to shape something new. Then transformation is stopped and you are held back from becoming your true self. You need to loosen the tight strings that hold your thinking and 'play' with new ways of seeing and being. Then you are able to extend beyond your current reach.

A new habit of thought, feeling or action must be sustained long enough for the old habit to fall away. When held and nourished over time, it begins to take practical shape and destruction of the old happens automatically. As part of the process you must be willing to let go of old ways of thinking.

Rather than hanging onto the branch and crying for freedom, the bird can fly when it lets go.

"It is an art to renounce. Certain things have to be given up. One of our spiritual efforts is to give up what is bad in us. Those who have learned this art are able to give them up easily, quickly. Those who have not learned this art give up some bad habits but carry others or they lower the intensity of a bad habit but are not able to eradicate it from their life." Br. Jagdish Chandra

Invitation to Contemplate and Write:

- *Recall a time when you embraced a new way of thinking about someone or something and everything changed for the benefit of all? What happened? What helped you open up to something new?*

- *What are the powers and virtues you have been developing on your spiritual path?*
- *What are some natural qualities you have revealed in yourself as you re-programmed your thinking habits?*
- *What helps you break illusions that you realize are no longer healthy for you or anyone else?*
- *What barriers do you face now in transforming how you show up in the world? Is the real you stepping out today?*
- *What is the focus of transformation for you now?*

Setting an Intention for Learning: To practice transforming thoughts by stretching beyond the usual playgrounds of your thinking

Meditation

Introducing the Art of Transformation
The Art of Transformation is about changing perceptions, breaking illusions; bringing back into play long lost, hidden qualities (peace, purity, love, happiness, wisdom), powers and virtues that have lost a place in daily expression.

In this session, you will be asking your mind to look at situations through a variety of lenses. It is about bringing your best qualities forward to shift your awareness and vision so that something new can manifest. This art focuses on re-shaping the mind and its thought processes. You will play and experiment with new ways of looking at the world around you and use your innate qualities and powers from deep inside to see what lies clearly beyond the illusion, beneath the surface – visual, auditory and mental.

You will stretch your mind and your habits of thinking beyond their usual 'playgrounds'. The soul that drives each body has an amazing capacity to shed old, outmoded ways of thinking and transform them. Soul consciousness permits going beyond limitations of the mind to new realms of possibility in thoughts and beliefs, leading to new patterns of behavior. Worry, fear and sadness drop away and you develop a new appreciation of who you really are.

Experiencing the Art of Transformation
There are several experiments in this session that ask you to transform habitual patterns of thinking.

Experiment #1
Take your journal and in a minute of silence, recall a time or situation when you realized that your way of thinking about the situation no longer served you. In fact, you were aware of wasting your time and energy by continuing to think in this way.

Describe the situation, what your usual thoughts were, what was shifting and what was required of you to make the shift?

Put this aside and we will come back to it at the end of the session.

Experiment #2
This is *a riddle*. Riddles are often used to help children think and see things differently.
A. "What is greater than God, worse than evil, the poor have it, the rich require it, and if you eat it, you die?"

Work on it if you haven't heard it before. Do not go to the answer right away. Check how you are feeling about doing this kind of thinking. See answer at the end of session.

Consider another riddle:
B. You have a fox, a chicken and a sack of grain. You must cross a river with only one of them at a time. If you leave the fox with the chicken he will eat it; if you leave the chicken with the grain he will eat it. How can you get all three across safely?

Again, work on it if you haven't heard it before. Do not go to the answer right away. Check how you are feeling about doing this kind of thinking. See answer at the end of session.

Experiment #3
Here are some brainteasers:
C. Connect the dots using one continuous line; do not lift your pen from the paper.

•   •   •

•   •   •

•   •   •

Again, work on it if you haven't seen it before. Do not go to the answer right away. Check how you are feeling about doing this kind of thinking. See answer at the end of session.

Experiment #4
Choose a card from the deck of self-mastery cards or virtue cards. Look at yourself in a mirror or look at a photo of someone through that virtue. (In a group look at someone sitting near you). After 3 minutes, choose another card and look at the same person through the lens of a different virtue. Choose another card if you are inclined. (In a group, look at the person sitting on your left through that virtue.)

What was surprising about this exercise? How did choosing a different 'lens' affect what you saw?

Experiment #5
A coloring exercise: you will need crayons for this one.
Be relaxed and put your mind into a meditative state with your eyes open and colour this picture of an elephant (picture and web-site below). The rules are to start at the top and stay within the lines. Notice what happens after a few minutes and watch as your mind understands the challenges in this experiment and decides how to reconcile the situation.

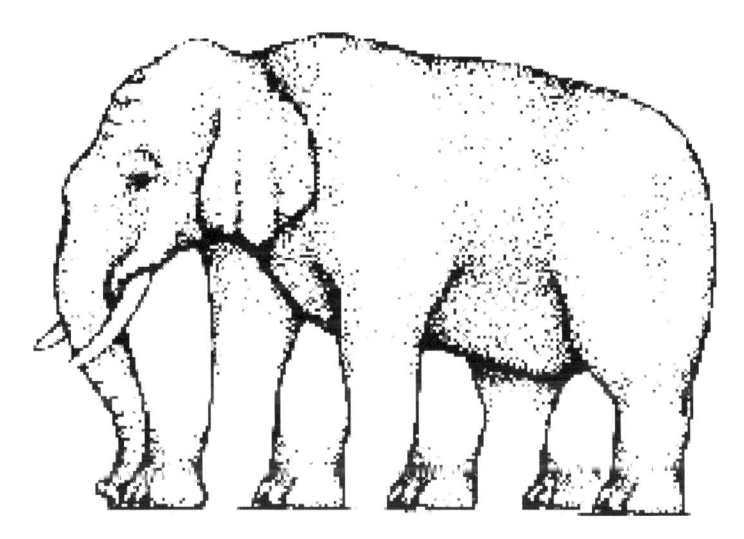

How is this exercise symbolic of experiences in life?

Reflecting on the Experience (Awareness)
Review the 3 experiments – the riddles, the brain-tester and the colouring activity:
- In which experiment were you most aware of being asked to transform your way of seeing and thinking about what was in front of you?
- How easy or difficult was that for you? How is this like the situation you noted in your journal as you began the session?
- Did your attitude shift? If so, how did it happen? What helped you reshape or transform your first perceptions?

Valuing the Art of Transformation (Attitude)
- What is one insight that could shift your thinking about a situation in your life right now?
- What is one significant check you can perform to ensure you are seeing the whole picture or thinking in the most beneficial way possible in the situation?

Embodying the Art of Transformation (Action)
In meditation, we use the acronym SOS – Stop Observe Steer to remind us to choose a lens that will help change 'waste thoughts to best'.

- After your reflections, choose one lens that you would like to use this week to shift your awareness, attitudes, vision from waste to best.

Closing
Complementary song/music to the art.

Resources and References
- Journal
- Crayons for colouring
- Elephant picture from http://www.123opticalillusions.com – use the elephant leg illusion for drawing and others for fun if you like.
- Answers to riddles:
  A. 'nothing'
  B. *Take the chicken, then the fox. Bring the chicken back and take the grain. Then go back and get the chicken.*

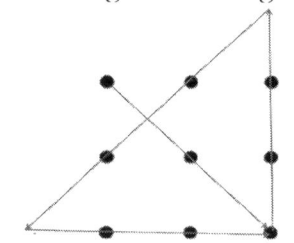

C.

Living as Art: Leisure and Work

"To work with yourself and what is around you, is the beginning. Then desires and duty become one."
Anthea Church

Work and leisure are partners in life. Some believe that only when the work is complete can leisure time be taken. However, when the work never ends, when do we enjoy leisure?

Hurry and finish work so you can rest.

Rush to get to the moment in the day when you can relax.

Rush through your work life until the time comes to retire.

The art of work and leisure is the capacity to blend the best of work and leisure in everything you do, knowing they are equal. Can work be done in a leisurely manner ~ without losing the high quality reserved for the attentiveness of work? Would the quality of input at work increase if the mind was at rest?

"Work and leisure are separate, because inside there is separation. It is a time of fragments, looking at each thing isolated and strengthening it until it's time to bring all of it together and when that happens, when all things converge, completed, then everyone in our orbit will move together too. And that is the beginning of unity. And in unity, work and leisure are one, for nothing needs to be singled out and mastered – which is work, and nothing needs to be relaxed and nurtured – which is leisure, for everything is equal and has its place."
Anthea Church

When you know how to work you rely on your own capacity to get things done. This creates a false sense of control over situations. Then work becomes tense due to an over-focus on outcomes. When work is done in a leisurely but careful way, more gets done ~ quicker and with more accuracy. This is because there are fewer mishaps caused by tension.

Work or leisure is a state of consciousness.

On the spiritual journey we learn to understand the power of pure intention to get things done. Of course there are still actions to perform, deadlines to be met but we understand that an aim filled with God's energy adds power to any job, and gets results without labour. Our focus then, shifts from outcome to input as we ensure the highest quality energy is put into every task.

"Every action has a feeling within it. Either we are doing something out of compulsion or duty or we do everything gladly. It is the art of spirituality to do everything gladly. Even if I don't feel like doing something, I do it anyways and I put happiness into every action. Then others are grateful and appreciative because you have added additional value to the action with your spiritual vibrations and happy feeling. Otherwise mentally and physically we become sick and the person we are doing something for also becomes sick. Then we infect others with our attitude." Br. Jagdish Chandra

To do everything in a leisurely way means to bring a sense of enjoyment to every minute. In soul conscious awareness you can invest the highest quality energy into each action and thought. Then the contrast between work and leisure is not so stark. And you no longer need as much leisure time because you are not tired.

"If you feel too tired to walk with others or accompany them to work, instead of staying in bed to rest, come and stand at the gate and smile with happiness as you send them off with good wishes. Then they are happy to see you because you have contributed happiness to the task. People are amazed when they see the happy faces of servers here. No one is tired; everyone has a smile on their face." Br. Jagdish Chandra

There is always an abundance of energy to do the things that interest you. When that which interests you also serves the best interest of others, work becomes a vocation. Then, because your core motivational energy is involved, you become tireless. This is the art of work and leisure.

Invitation to Contemplate and Write:

- *Remember a time when true self shone through - at work or in your leisure hours?*
- *Which comes first for you - leisure or work? Why?*
- *How clearly can work and leisure time be separated?*
- *What activities meant for self-actualization can be found in your work and your leisure?*
- *Where in your life does the separation between work and leisure get blurred? Is it OK?*
- *What is your intention when you consider how you spend your time for leisure and for work?*

Setting an Intention for Learning: To spiritualize our understandings of leisure and work

Meditation

Introducing the Art of Leisure and Work
In the 1970's, at a time when innovation and automation were introduced into people's lives at home and at work, futurists predicted there would be much more leisure time for recreational pursuits! It was thought that this surplus of leisure time would allow women, freed from the burden of domestic chores, to play a more active role in community decision-making. And men could be more involved in parenting. Somehow these engendered notions of work and leisure have found little truth 50 years later.

Later, the creation of computers and other smart devices promised the end of work. Again we wondered what we would do with all our leisure time. However, we have not seen this to be the case. The motivation behind many of our inventions and technology was to free us from work and yet the work continues to increase. Why is this?

In this session we will explore the spiritual side of work and leisure at this time in human history.

Experiencing the Art of Leisure and Work
Imagine a day, wherein you actually spent an hour in a way that was perfect for you.

Now imagine yourself sitting back in contemplation after that perfect hour and reflecting on the virtue or power you experienced during that perfect hour – *what was your feeling and the quality in your soul that was expressed*?

Draw a picture that represents this feeling and the expression of this quality. Once you are finished, turn the piece of paper over. We will use it for another drawing on the back very soon.

Now consider how you define or understand these two concepts: work and leisure. What does 'work' mean to you? What words come to mind when you think about work? List these words or phrases in a left-hand column on a separate piece of paper.

What does 'leisure mean'? What words describe it? Write them on the right column of the paper.

Looking at what you have written, what is one simple way of differentiating between work and leisure? Write a definition that works for you. Set this aside.

There are 7 quick steps in this activity.
1. Return to the back side of the paper with your ideal hour on it. *Draw a circle* in the centre of the page taking up about ¼ of the diameter of the page. Make it into a 24-hour clock, with 0:00 hr. at the top, 6 hr. at the right, 12 hr. at the bottom and 18 hr. at the left coming around to 24 hours.
2. **Divide the day** – today specifically not a general day or a good day – **today.** How did you spend your time today? Mark lines where you changed activities. For example, the hours between 22 hr. and 4 hr. could be 6-hours of sleep, 4 - 7:30 hr. could be meditation, etc. All around the clock.
3. Now draw a second circle outside the first and mark it off in the months of the year January at the top, March on the right, July on the bottom, October on the left back to December ending at the top.
4. Draw a third circle outside the second and mark it off in an average lifespan of 84 years with birth 1 at the top, 21 on the right, 42 at the bottom, 63 at the left and coming around to 84 at the top again. (For a BK audience, you also could do a fourth circle of 84 births).
5. Now *choose two colors of crayons* and using the definition of work and leisure generated earlier – choose one colour to represent work and the other to represent leisure.
6. Put a star representing the soul in the centre of the first circle.
7. Draw lines from the centre out through each activity you have marked from today and extend it out to the month circle

and the year circles, making a large pie chart. As you do this decide whether each activity is work or leisure and colour each slice of time accordingly.

(In a group, before any discussion, have everyone *pass their chart* around in silence and let everyone view each chart that has been created.)

Reflecting on the Experience (Awareness)
- What did you notice during this activity? Was there a moment that caught your attention? What happened in that moment?
- What does this chart suggest about how you balance work and leisure in your life?
- Given your description of a perfect hour, what are 2 ways you could turn this current day into a perfect day?

Valuing the Art of Leisure and Work (Attitude)
- What activities add value to how you spend a day? Does it translate well to a month, a year, a lifetime?
- What are you happy to see gets the value it deserves?
- What is one area you would like to see valued more using time as a measure in your circles?

Embodying the Art of Leisure and Work (Action)
- Imagine stepping into the centre of this chart and experiencing your energy radiating outwards through your life. Imagine this energy creating a perfect whether at work or in leisure.
- Make a determined thought to hold this awareness this week.

Closing
Complementary song/music to the art.

Resources and References
None.

Living as Art: Maintaining Equanimity

Equanimity is inner balance.
Equanimity reflects inner neutrality in the face of multiple and/or opposing views. It is emotional stability as a result of non-attachment.

We live in a world of many ideas. Each idea is valid in its own context. However, we have developed the habit of giving greater value to one idea over another, based on perception and preference.

Dualism means 'two ways'. There is your way and my way, this way and that way. However, when we charge one way with positive energy and the other with negative energy; polarity is born. Polarity is 'having poles or polar opposites'. Polarity is experienced as a push and pull of energy ~ within a situation, between two people or within a person.

The inner push and pull of polarity results in an imbalance in attitude and awareness which creates actions that are off-balance. We can say too much and wish later we had been silent. Or we do too much and feel 'over-responsible' and resentful.

Most of us are accustomed to living with polarities such as:
- say something or remain quiet
- go out or stay in
- take the lead or wait and see
- invest more or leave
- do or be
- Yin/Yang
- Masculine/Feminine

Although we understand that neither is better or worse, we are taken off-balance when these energies conflict inside us. Each situation requires a different energetic response. Balance is the act of centering oneself at the pivot point between two contrasting energies, to walk the fine line between too much and too little, too late and too early. To balance means to be stable and 'centered', not pushed or pulled in any direction. This is the art of maintaining equanimity.

In spirituality, we consider ***balancing opposites*** as those qualities that seem opposing but have equal value. Some examples include:
- Master/Child
- Loveful/Lawful
- Silence/Sound
- Physical/Subtle

To be complete is to be both at the same time, to have within you the energy of both e.g. masculine and feminine and to access each as needed, integrating both energies within the self in a balanced way.

When spiritually complete, a soul is free from the push and pull of old habits, beliefs, hurts and desires. In a state of inner fullness, the soul is free from the confusion, chaos or inner conflict experienced in polarity and lives the perfect balance of 'both/and' rather than 'either/or'.

Spirituality teaches you to raise your consciousness above the push and pull of polarity.

Rising above polarity you are then able to re-set your energy at the highest vibration. You understand that the only way to fully integrate your inner polarities is to tether your consciousness to the highest energy in the universe.

To maintain perfect balance it is necessary to anchor your consciousness within, on the point (soul) and beyond, to the Point (Supreme Soul). When your energy is right, a balanced, artful action will follow.

The Art of Maintaining Equanimity is the spiritual stance required to go beyond opposing energies, thus harmonizing the self with the highest all-benevolent energy of the One.

Invitation to Contemplate and Write:

- *Remember a time when you could fully embrace the two sides of the same coin ~ when you could see both sides with equanimity?*
- *What are the daily situations that create a 'push/pull' effect in you – a like/dislike, or good/bad judgment?*
- *When you experience the push/pull effect inside you ~ is it about people, priorities, values or beliefs?*
- *What happens to your energy in these situations?*
- *What does it mean to be able to consider both without needing to choose?*
- *What is your aim when confronted with dualism or polarity?*

Setting an Intention for Learning: To explore ways of maintaining equanimity in life.

Meditation

Introducing the Art of Maintaining Equanimity
Equanimity is not a word we use often in everyday language and yet it is deeply desired by those who are learning to meditate. Consider the following definitions:

- *Equanimity* comes from the combination of "aequus" and "animus" ("soul" or "mind") in the Latin phrase aequo animo, which means "with even mind"
- fairness, impartiality from the French 'equanimite'
- mental calmness, composure, and evenness of temper, especially in a difficult situation

Experiencing the Art of Maintaining Equanimity
Life sometimes has highs, sometimes lows, sometimes praise, sometimes insults, sometimes abundance and sometimes scarcity. Consider: how is it useful to maintain equanimity in the face of life's challenges?

In this session, you have the opportunity to explore equanimity through 5 short experiments.

Experiment #1
Place a line of tape on the floor, name one side A and the other side B. Stand on the tape.

Read the list of word pairs below and choose the one you like best of each pair you are presented with. Return to the tape after each choice and start from the center place for the next selection.

A	B
Volleyball	Football
Beach	Mountains
Hot weather	Cold weather
Barefoot	Shoes
Long hair	Short hair
Red	Yellow

In your journal consider:
- How was your experience? Were all the choices easy? Were some more difficult than others? Why?
- What do you notice about the reasons behind your choices? (in a group hear comments)

Experiment #2

Using the same process with tape on the floor, consider another set of choices we are confronted with throughout the day, what is your usual preference?

A	B
Stay home	Go out
Say something	Remain quiet
Take the lead	Follow someone's lead
Caffeine boost	No Caffeine
Be on time	Be a little late
Walk	Take the car

- How was your experience with those choices? Were all the choices easy? Were some more difficult than others? Why?
- What do you notice about the reasons behind your choices? (hear comments)

Experiment #3

What are some other choices that push and pull you throughout the day? Put them on the A/B chart and consider your preferences.

Consider again:
- Were all the choices easy? Were some more difficult than others? Why?

- What do you notice about the reasons behind your choices?
- What do you notice about the types of choices?
- What does this suggest about the experience of push and pull that challenges equanimity?

Experiment #4

Using the chart below, consider a socially acceptable quality such as 'telling the truth'. Push yourself with this chart – even though it may be easy to consider the positives of this quality, you will be asked to consider the negatives. Push yourself further and consider the negative aspects of the positive factors and the positive factors related to the negatives! Try it!

Consider "Telling the truth"	
Step 1 What is positive about this?	**Step 3** What could be negative about these positive aspects?
A. B. C.	For A. For B. For C.
Step 2 What could be negative about this?	**Step 4** What could be positive about these negative aspects?
D. E. F.	For D. For E. For F.

- What did you notice about your feelings as you progressed through the different stages of this charting?
- When did you experience it to be easy? Why? What was difficult? Why?
- What is important when maintaining equanimity in the face of positive and negative?

Experiment #5

For this last activity, consider one of your 'best' qualities. It should be a quality you feel good about being able to use practically in your life. It may be a quality for which you receive compliments from others. Use the same chart and consider this quality more fully.

I am _____	
Step 1 What is positive about this quality?	**Step 3** What could be negative about the positive aspects?
A. B. C.	For A. For B. For C.
Step 2 What is negative about this quality?	**Step 4** What could be positive about the negative aspects?
D. E. F.	For D. For E. For F.

- What did you notice about your feelings as you progressed through the different stages of this charting?
- When did you experience it to be easy? Why? What was difficult? Why?
- What does this suggest about working with equanimity in the face of 'good' qualities?

Reflecting on the Experience (Awareness)
- What was challenging as you worked through the 5 experiments related to maintaining equanimity?
- What was surprising to you? What was inspiring to you?

Valuing the Art of Maintaining Equanimity (Attitude)
- What did you learn about maintaining equanimity?
- What is important to remember for maintaining equanimity?
- What was significant in this session that will influence your spiritual journey?

Embodying the Art of Maintaining Equanimity (Action)
- What is one intention you will practice this week related to maintaining equanimity?

Closing
Complementary song/music to the art.

Resources and References
- Tape
- Handouts if in group

Celebrating the Arts

When dreaming becomes doing,
your destination becomes destiny.

It is time to celebrate the beauty that has always been inside you and is now re-emerging.

Time is calling each of us to fulfill the potential buried inside. You may feel your potential pulling you. You may feel it pushing you. It will find expression.

It is time for the full potential of every soul to be expressed. This is a basic premise of Raja Yoga meditation.

Living life as art describes a natural way of being. Although it may have been forgotten, it calls to be discovered again. It is time to remember.

To remember is to recall something that
was known and forgotten.

In celebrating the end of sixteen sessions, we are really celebrating the emergence of the true self.

Every moment spent contemplating spiritual knowledge and creating a high awareness and attitude is precious ~ especially when it informs action. Then dreaming becomes doing.

Please consider the following quote:

"Always remember three expressions:
Always maintain a balance. 2) Always remain blissful. 3)
Give blessings to everyone. Let there always be
a balance between self-service and service of others.

So many talents are shown through a balance.

You will become 16 celestial degrees complete by maintaining the balance of your intellect. Every act you perform will become an art. Your way of seeing will be an art because you listen to and see everything as a soul. In the same way, let your way of speaking, your way of walking, etc., all be an art.

However, the basis of all of this is the balance of your intellect. To remain constantly blissful means to be an embodiment of bliss." Ayvakt Bapdada

Invitation to Contemplate and Write:

- *Remember a time when you felt whole, balanced and stable – what led to this feeling of fullness? What do you do that helps you hold on to it?*
- *What helps you create balance in what you do for yourself and what you do for others?*
- *What talent shines through you like an art?*
- *What is an art you hope to develop fully over the next year?*

Setting an Intention for Learning: To reflect on your personal experiences during the *Living as Art* series and celebrate living life as art.

Meditation

Introducing Celebrating
Each week for sixteen weeks, you have been immersed in experiments of living life as art. In this session, you will have a chance to reflect on the full series and re-discover your brilliance as symbolized by the moon, reflecting more light on its journey to fullness.

You are now in the phase between *dreaming* about what life can be and *doing* it -- living life as art. Your *dreaming* must always be elevated – desiring to do the best for yourself and others. Your *doing* must always be toward attaining the goal in such a way as to inspire others.

Experiencing Celebrating Living as Art
In this session there are two experiments to help reflect and celebrate Living as Art.

Experiment #1
Review and reflect - In your journal, take time to review what you have written during the sessions, which started with the introductory session and includes all sixteen arts.

After this review go to the list of arts in the introductory section of this book. Select one art that feels full and complete and shines brightly in you. Take a moment and give thanks for this art.

Then select another art in which you have made a lot of progress. Perhaps you understand it better or you feel it shining in you like a half moon or more? Again, give thanks for this art.

In your journal, write a letter to God, the Source of all that shines through you. Describe how these arts serve you in your life now and how they serve to inspire others.

Read your letter aloud to yourself. Notice how you feel.

Experiment #2
Dreaming to Doing - Review the list of 16 Arts again. This time choose two arts that intrigue you. They may feel distant, not part of your life experience so far, or you may feel uncertain about what the art is and how you can manifest it in your life to benefit self and others.

Sit quietly and be still. Dream an image of yourself with this art full and complete, shining brightly for all to witness.

In your dream, see the faces of two people who will be inspired by your new awareness and attitude as you fill your life with these arts.

Once their faces are clear to you, take out your journal and write a note to yourself about your dream of how you are living this art. Write about the positive influence it had on these two other souls.

Also select a date (one month from today) to check-in with these two people to ask if they noticed anything different in you. Check if it has had any effect on them. The idea being you will not share your dream with them, but will check-in specifically after a month to see if they noticed anything in you.

To help you during the month (and for future Living as Art experiments), here are some helpful tips:

Set Your Aim Daily
Set your aim at the beginning of the day or the night before. This ensures your time and efforts are used in a worth-while-way. Be *practical* and select specific ways you want to shine this art today.

Check and Change
Whenever you have a few moments, check how you've done so far in the day. *Reflect* on your aim and check how close you've come during the last few hours.

Plan Ahead: Be the Art
At the beginning of your day, block off the time you want for a specific thought and action toward your aim. Plan your activities for the entire day as well as your stage!

Be Honest
Be honest with yourself. Reflect and record what is truly in your heart, good or bad. Only then will you see your honest effort and what more is required.

Show and Tell
If you are comfortable with it, share how you are *progressing* and see what others have noticed.

Have Fun
Be creative. See what *newness* emerges in the self. Let this attention to Living as Art be a stepping stone for you to create your best you – full and complete.

Reflecting on the Experience (Awareness)
- What drew your attention during the celebrating Living as Art session ~ in each of the experiments? How vivid was your dream of Living as Art for your next steps?

Valuing Living as Art (Attitude)
- What is important about taking the time to celebrate Living as Art with review, reflection and looking ahead?

Embodying Living as Art (Action)
- Imagine taking your first steps this week toward an even better you. Love you. Remain balanced. Remain blissful. Give thanks to everyone along the way.

Closing
Complementary song/music to the art.

Back to the Beginning

Bravo! Congratulations! You have been living the life of an artist by spending time and effort to refine the daily activities that make living an art.

We hope you have enjoyed exploring the sixteen celestial degrees and that, in some small way; they have contributed to your growing sense of completeness.

By participating in this thoughtful exploration, you have offered yourself and your special talents to increase the positive vibrations in service of humanity and the creation of a better world.

You are now more familiar with what it takes to master essential elements of your everyday life. Hopefully the contemplative introduction and questions stimulated a degree of awareness enabling you to discover how full you feel in each of the arts.

By using the SERVE model[2] to reflect on your experiences with the arts, you have acquired awareness of an experiential learning approach to session designs. It can be used to create sessions to explore other 'arts'. In the context of today's world, there are many other activities that can benefit from an artful expression e.g. making decisions, organizing, letting go and so on.

---

[2] The design of the activity sessions is built around the five step SERVE model[2] of experiential learning:
- **S**et an intention for learning
- **E**xperience the Art
- **R**eflect on the experience (become more **AWARE** of the art)
- **V**alue the art (awaken a positive **ATTITUDE** towards the art)
- **E**mbody the art (consider ways to put it in **ACTION**)

Each soul has a unique part to play and the aim of completeness will require a different curriculum for each of us. You will find lists of other arts to explore in the resource section at the back of this book. They include the originals of Brother Jagdish and Anthea Church, as well as a contemporary list generated by two young people at university. These lists are offered as a starting point for your further reflection and experimentation.

We refine ourselves as artists of life when we remember that we are souls, tiny points of light energy using these bodies to express ourselves in the world while constantly and courageously connecting to God, the Divine Source of virtues and spiritual energy.

May others be inspired by your daily behaviour, just as Brother Jagdish was inspired when he observed the practical actions of Brahma Baba.

Acknowledgements

The conversations that created this book began in 2009 with friends at the BK meditation centre in Halifax. They continue to encourage experimentation with many aspects of spiritual knowledge and willingly offer themselves as 'guinea pigs' for new session designs.

A swirl of thought energy converged around the theme of the sixteen arts in the final months of 2017. Workshops were conducted in Madhuban during the winter season and many BK students around the world were actively investigating the arts at the time of our writing.

Heartfelt appreciations to all the spiritual friends who offered conversation, insights and suggestions during the preparation of the book ~ a special thanks to Gopi Patel, Frank Hubbard, Michael Timmons, Shuna Herscowitz and Dr. Murli.

Thank you to the Halifax clan who are always ready to experiment and especially Teri Crawford for her accurate editorial comments. Rachel Morgan offered great design ideas and Lucy Morgan offered her editorial eye and discerning intellect.

A warm thank you to Judi Rich who created the beautiful cover design.

A sweet appreciation to Br. Jagdish whose churnings and writings continue to inspire.

And a special note of gratitude to Anthea Church for writing in a way that touches the heart and gently pries it open. And for your willingness to accompany this project to its completion with all the emails of support and encouragement.

And thank you to all of you who are making efforts to be the best human being possible.

"Victory is guaranteed!" said the Sun to the Moon.

Resources and Reference Material

A List of Virtues

Cheerful • Powerful • Transformative • Positive • Creative

Mature • Stabile • Balanced • Honest • Polite

Spontaneous • Compassionate • Tireless • Gentle • Truthful

Introspective • Strong • Healing • Accurate • Peaceful • Patient

Generous • Enthusiastic • Cooperative • Flexible • Open • Content

Courageous • Resourceful • Happy • Pure-Hearted

Adventurous • Constant • Trusting • Self-Confident • Forgiving

Practical • Determined • Magical • Responsible • Detached

Sweet • Centered • Calm • Intuitive • Nurturing • Dignified

Wisdom • Wonder • Respect • Tolerance • Silence • Discipline

Beauty • Concentration • Humour • Purpose • Delight

Acceptance • Knowledge • Simplicity • Appreciation • Humility

Serenity • Self-Respect • Love • Determination • Empowerment

Easiness • Communication • Forgiveness • Freedom • Integrity

Br. Jagdish Chandra
16 Celestial Degrees

Art of Relaxation
If we live our life with the definite belief that the supreme soul is the real director and actor and we are only His instruments we can always remain contented and relaxed even in illness. The knowledge that this is all an account of our own past deeds enables us to be stable in varying situations viewing them as various scenes of the pre-destined world drama. The picture of Vishnu with the serpent bed in the ocean is symbolic of the art of relaxation.

Art of Dealing or Behaviour
Our behaviour towards all should be such that it is full of natural and selfless love, respect, divine family feeling and sweetness. Such a person easily wins over every ones' heart and rules over it. It is said that handsome is that which handsome does.

Art of Keeping Healthy
Health (Swasth in Hindi) means 'swa' (= soul/self) performing all deeds in soul conscious stage it is the key to be healthy. By considering ourselves as kings of anxiety-less land we can always remain happy because there is no diet comparable to happiness. Clean drinking water, fresh food and fresh air have important place in maintaining good health. Baba used to say that for maintaining healthy and happy go on earning good wishes of all along with proper meditation and medication. Understanding the deep secret of drama and remaining happy in all situations ~ is the art of keeping healthy.

Art of Teaching
The Adi Pita Brahma Baba with his sweet actions, loving spiritual vision, positive attitude and behaviour used to teach the children the lesson of belongingness. The essence of the art of teaching is loveful behaviour. Saint Kabir Das has said this in his

meaningful words – "Studying books after books, the world has passed by, none has become really knowledgeable. One who learns the short word (love) becomes truly knowledgeable."

Though there are four subjects in Raja Yoga, Baba used to teach it in such a way as if he was teaching a single subject and was teaching it like a story. There used to be intimacy between the teacher and the student. If he had to point out some weakness to anyone, he used to do so individually in private and when he had to praise anybody, he used do it openly in front of all due to which his self-respect always remained intact and he used to transform himself. Sri Krishna's teaching to Arjuna while sitting on the chariot represents this art of teaching.

Art of Letter Writing
Baba's letters used to be the source of inspiration in everybody's life. If Baba was to draw anyone's attention towards any of his deficiency, then he would first shower praises on him, then point out his deficiency in a symbolic (beautiful) way so that he would not feel himself degraded. Baba's letters created desire for repeated reading. Baba used to win others through his letters. On reading his letters, the soul used to surrender itself to him.

The Art of Sustenance
Like a mother, Baba used to bring up and guide the children with great love, sacrifice, service and with tirelessness. Baba used to say, "Do not take rest after holding an exhibition, fair or doing any other service; follow it up, then there would be result. If some seeker does not come due to some reason, send 'murli' or a letter or some 'prasad' (sweet) or allot him some service, then he would keep on coming in contact.

Art of Marching Ahead
Our goal in life should always be elevated and we should go on making efforts to attain that goal. Whatever challenges (tests) come on the way, always go on marching ahead. Our progress would become a source of inspiration for others too.

Art of Entertainment
Baba used to entertain and make children laugh while imparting knowledge. He used to clarify several deep secrets of knowledge in a very easy and entertaining manner. He used to cross adverse situations very happily. Baba used to entertain and make children occasionally laugh and would say, "Always keep on smiling like flowers."

Art of Sweet Talking
There is a saying "The tongue can bestow one with a throne, or can also lead one to the gallows". With sweet words, a person crosses many difficult situations. In a soul-conscious stage, a person always speaks sweet words. A poet has truly said:
'A sweet word is a medicine and
a bitter word is an arrow;
it affects the entire body
though the hearing path is narrow.'

The Art of Making One's Own
Baba used to fill so much confidence in children by loving and praising them that their virtues began to develop and they used to perform wonders. Baba used to fill hope in hopeless souls. He used to win over other's hearts in such a way that they never desired to stay away from Baba. On meeting Baba everyone used to feel very light and happy.

The Art of Leadership
A leader's task is to awaken people and encourage them to progress. Baba brought every effort-maker into active service as per their qualities so that he could develop his/her potentiality. When the intellect is engaged in creative activity, the destructive activities automatically cease. As a stone becomes worship-worthy when rolling (being smoothed and polished) with the current of the water, similarly by serving others, gradually a person becomes valuable gems.

The Art of Learning
Learning implies transformation in one's life. Brahma Baba, even after attaining old age, always used to consider himself just a student. This attitude took him to the peak of the heights.

Learning needs inquisitiveness. Baba, while explaining the importance of spiritual education, used to say, 'Children who love the murli also love the Murlidhar (Deliverer of the murli). Therefore never miss morning class of Murli (spiritual discourse).' Similarly when Baba used to address even old persons as 'children' they also acquired alertness for learning and study.

The Art of Transformation or Moulding
Baba used to say that after understanding one's duty and aim of life, it is not difficult to mould oneself and transforming one's life style and the old sanskaras (habits). In Brahma Baba's own life, such transformation was evident. The day he experienced the vision 'I am Vishnu so are you', from that very day the transformation started taking place. Quick efforts mean quick transformation, i.e., 'immediate charity results in great achievements.' Baba adopted this technique in his life as a great formula.

The Art of Changing Waste into Best
People convert waste iron or gold into new articles by melting. Similarly, after making others to give up their old sanskars (tendencies) and old habits, Baba used to inspire them to transform these into good habits. He always upheld the pious thought to transform the vicious world into vice less. Baba also used to transform some old useless things in the yagya into some new useful things.

The Art of Administration
For establishing the New World, transforming each and everyone's sanskars and habits is necessary which is really a difficult task. The greatest artist or administrator is one who can complete a task with minimum means. Baba's motto was 'Begin the job and means will automatically start coming by themselves.' Baba always used to give an opportunity to everyone to do something or the other. Baba's administration was so excellent that everybody demanded work because everyone saw the work as service and service as the basis for future rewards/achievement. Here, there is neither any supervisory nor any manager and nobody to show his ego or might. That is why,

in this administration, there is never any strike of work or a holiday. Every day, the class of Murli (learning) takes place at a punctual time.

The Art of Absorbance

It was observed in Baba's life that if any child put his/her confidence in Baba, Baba would absorb his weakness like an ocean and never expressed it to others. As such, everyone used to relate his/her mental agony to Baba with an open mind. Ganeshji is shown with a big belly as the symbol of the art of absorbance.

Anthea Church ~ The Arts of Living

The Art of Learning and Teaching
*When the mind is clean, supple and open, the learning comes
When teaching begins with love, it fills the atmosphere, and anyone can do anything.*

The Art of Communicating
When a word is as fragrant as a garden, a conversation is as refreshing as a walk.

The Art of Administration
To administer well, you need to know yourself deeply and let the harmony inside shine out. It is very personal.

The Art of Leading
To harbour a flawless quality inside of you, to preserve, nurture and use it at the time it is most needed, so that it is the quality that leads, not you.

The Art of Dealing with Others
To make room for and enjoy someone's whole world, no matter how complex, cluttered or twisted it may be, and to do this with grace and equanimity and to do this for everyone.

The Art of Organizing
To understand the bones of a task but also have a feel for the combination of qualities which, when brought together, can accomplish it.

The Art of Developing
The more vulnerable and changing you are, the more you need a task that is fixed.

The Art of Keeping Secrets
Seek perfection in private; even if you wished to, you couldn't speak a secret before its time for if you did, no one would hear.

The Art of Thinking and Creating
When the atmosphere is right, creation can take place. When a mind meets God, something great is created.

The Art of Remaining Contented and Happy
A life lived in contentment can inspire everyone and be possessed by no one... but you. It is yours alone.

The Art of Serving and Helping
You don't need any resources to serve from the heart, but you need to be rich inside.

The Art of Work & Leisure
To work with yourself and what is around you, is the beginning. Desires and duty become one.

The Art of Keeping Others Contented and Happy
When a King can become a child and a child a teacher – when letting go of roles is as easy as letting someone else have the ball

The Art of Reforming
The courage to lay still & awake, watching the surgeon work on you to remove something unwanted.

The Art of Winning Friends
Friendship is to sit in someone's mind and be at peace – with nothing in between.

The Art of Refreshing
The resource inside of you which can wash over the immediate and ordinary surface and bring something different to it

Create Your Own

Perhaps you have your own list of sixteen arts ~ those that represent the balanced expression of spiritual wholeness for you.

Here is a short list generated by two young adults when asked what arts they felt they needed to master at university:

1. The Art of Making Decisions (how to know the right thing to do?)
2. The Art of Giving (what is enough? too much? not enough?)
3. The Art of Being Glue (how to keep things/people/views together?)
4. The Art of Challenging Yourself (how to stretch for learning and not break?)
5. The Art of Making & Keeping Friends
6. The Art of Closing Things Well (using the past as a place of reference, not of residence but how to end things and move on gracefully?)
7. The Art of Letting Go (how to handle situations when you don't have control, accepting no control?)
8. The Art of Resolving Conflict/Disagreements
9. The Art of Engagement: Individual and Collective (a manual for interacting with the world)
10. The Art of Being Grateful (how to appreciate what's happening and what you have)

11. The Art of Apologizing (when to say sorry and how to do so while maintaining your self-respect?)
12. The Art of Keeping Perspective (how to right-size yourself and the situation so you don't get overwhelmed and can manage things?)
13. The Art of Following Rules (how to know what is most important in each situation - the spirit of the law or the letter of the law?)
14. The Art of Making Effort (understanding effort and return)
15. The Art of Managing Pressure (learning how to respond to new responsibilities and challenges that can be overwhelming)
16. The Art of Being Carefree (how to manage crazy thoughts and a mind full of worry?)

Made in the USA
Middletown, DE
22 January 2018